Effects, Applications and Future Scope of Recent Advances in Healthcare and Education Sectors

Effects, Applications and Future Scope of Recent Advances in Healthcare and Education Sectors

Edited by
Manisha Vohra

CWP
Central West Publishing

This edition has been published by Central West Publishing, Australia

For more information about the books published by Central West Publishing, please visit https://centralwestpublishing.com

Disclaimer
Every effort has been made by the publisher, editors and authors while preparing this book, however, no warranties are made regarding the accuracy and completeness of the content. The publisher, editors and authors disclaim without any limitation all warranties as well as any implied warranties about sales, along with fitness of the content for a particular purpose. Citation of any website and other information sources does not mean any endorsement from the publisher, editors and authors. For ascertaining the suitability of the contents contained herein for a particular lab or commercial use, consultation with the subject expert is needed. In addition, while using the information and methods contained herein, the practitioners and researchers need to be mindful for their own safety, along with the safety of others, including the professional parties and premises for whom they have professional responsibility. To the fullest extent of law, the publisher, editors and authors are not liable in all circumstances (special, incidental, and consequential) for any injury and/or damage to persons and property, along with any potential loss of profit and other commercial damages due to the use of any methods, products, guidelines, procedures contained in the material herein.

NATIONAL LIBRARY OF AUSTRALIA

A catalogue record for this book is available from the National Library of Australia

ISBN (print): 978-1-922617-30-9

About the Book

Education and healthcare sectors are two very vital sectors of the society. These sectors serve the society in various ways. The development and progress and of these sectors is always essential and of great importance. This book titled Effects, Applications and Future Scope of Recent Advances in Education and Healthcare Sectors, is a resourceful collection of book chapters explaining the applications, effects as well as future scope of recent advances in education and healthcare sectors which are largely due to evolution of different technologies. Also, the implementation of different technologies in these sectors in the form of different innovative ideas and solutions have contributed to the recent advances which ultimately lead towards the path of development and progress of education and healthcare sectors.

Manisha Vohra

Contents

1

Introduction of Artificial Intelligence in Education Sector

N. Karuppiah[a], S. Rajalingam[b], S. Tamilselvi[c] and J. Shanmugapriyan[d]

[a]*Vardhaman College of Engineering, Hyderabad, Telangana, India*
[b]*Sunyani Technical University, Ghana, West Africa*
[c]*Sri Sivasubramaniya Nadar College of Engineering, Chennai, India*
[d]*NSN College of Engineering and Technology, Karur, Tamil Nadu, India*

Abstract

Education is one of the best practices as it helps to learn skills and gain knowledge. It is the acquisition of knowledge and skills. Education sector is thus one of the most important sectors for the society. Introduction of Artificial Intelligence (AI) in education sector has paved way for transforming the education sector. This chapter discusses and explains the introduction of AI in education sector. This chapter will help in understanding what changes AI can bring in is the education sector.

1. Introduction

The use of Artificial Intelligence (AI) in education sector is currently progressing at an accelerated pace. AI has a major impact on education. It is an effective tool for disseminating knowledge globally.

AI is proving to be highly helpful in education sector. AI is helping the students to learn things online at any time and from any location. AI can help to bring an interactive method of learning for students. Personalized Learning can be facilitated to the students using AI.

The curriculum can be taught in different ways to the students using AI. In addition to this, AI can also assist the teachers in their work. For example, AI can help the teachers in doing analysis of the results of students by conducting tests online, assessing the test automatically, grading answer sheets, etc.

2. Role of AI in education sector

The role of AI in the educational sector is analyzed under five parameters namely

Interaction
Teaching content
Approach of teaching
Evaluation
Detailed result analysis

2.1 Interaction

The education of the students can be carried out well only when there is interaction between the students and the teachers. It is essential to have proper student-teacher interaction. Interactive communication between the students and the teacher is an integral part of the learning system which facilitates learning.

AI can also help in providing an interactive learning environment for the students. An intelligent tutoring system based on AI can provide an interactive learning environment that helps the students in understanding and learning the different curriculum concepts being taught.

2.2 Teaching content

Teaching content refers to the things that the students require to learn during their course of study and is called curriculum. AI can play a great role in framing the curriculum pertaining to the needs of the student and industry.

It can also help to assess the student's knowledge via various online tests which can be helpful to learn the framed curriculum in the stipulated period of time.

2.3 Approach of teaching

The next important part is the approach of teaching adopted by the teachers to make the students learn. The teachers can decide and have any approach of teaching as they find it appropriate for teaching. However, AI can replace the common conventional part of the approach of teaching.

For example, writing on the blackboard with chalk during explaining curriculum concepts to students is one of the common part of any approach that is many times adopted by the teachers. This is not a compulsory part, but a common part of any approach adopted by the teachers during teaching which can be replaced by using AI tools and in recent times, where education is being conducted online, smart classrooms with different AI tools are being introduced to facilitate learning. Teachers, with the help of AI, can design effective teaching approach for the students.

2.4 Evaluation

Evaluation is a process carried out by the teachers to assess the learning outcome of the students during their course of study. It is a tool used to evaluate the understanding of different subjects taught in the curriculum to students at different time intervals of their study.

Based on the evaluated results, the teachers are able to identify how well the students have understood the curriculum concepts taught to them and are able to guide them effectively. With AI, evaluation can be easily done using online automated evaluation options.

2.5 Detailed result analysis

Even after evaluation, a detailed analysis of the result is required to understand better the performance of the students in exams. This detailed analysis can guide the teachers in their future approach as well as the students in deciding their study plan.

AI can help in this case by carrying out a detailed analysis of the result and can present the detailed analysis to the students and teachers. As mentioned above, this detailed analysis can thus guide the teachers in their future approach in teaching and it can guide the students in deciding their studying plan based on the detailed result analysis.

3. Advancements in education sector facilitating the introduction and use of AI in education

Technological advancements in education sector have already facilitated the use of various ICT tools as well as different digital applications for teaching and learning curriculum concepts. The traditional method of writing on the blackboard and teaching has changed to quite an extent.

ICT tools such as smartphone, tablet, laptops, etc. are being utilized for easing and making the teaching-learning process better, especially during the pandemic, the usage of ICT tools for teaching-learning process has increased.

Along with it, different digital applications are also being used in teaching-learning process and since the pandemic, its usage in education sector has also increased. Below is the example and description of few such ICT tools and digital applications and software that are being included in education sector.

3.1 ICT tools in education sector

ICT tools are helpful and effective in educational learning and teaching. Some of the commonly used ICT tools are Smart Phone, Tablet, Laptop/Desktop, Interactive whiteboard, etc. Now ICT tools have become a vital part of the educational teaching-learning process. They have replaced approaches like traditional blackboard with interactive digital whiteboards, tablets, smartphones and other related electronic gadgets [2].
The usage of ICT tools is helping the students and teachers. Some of the ICT tools frequently used in the education sector are as follows.

Smartphones and Tablets

Smartphone and tablets are one of the ICT tools that have made their mark and is being used for education. One of their advantages is that, they are portable devices with amazing features.
Smartphones and tablets for learning and teaching process, helps the students and teachers to get all the necessary educational information quickly.

Projectors

Projectors enable to display PowerPoint presentations, animations, videos and other relevant materials related to the curriculum concepts for teaching which will be helpful for the students in learning.

Laptops/Desktops

It is one of the most common tools used in the education sector. It can be utilized for studying, teaching, preparing notes, etc. Students and teachers can also share study assignments and do collaborative educational work through this tool. It helps to develop various digital skills.

Interactive White Board

This is also known as the electronic whiteboard. It can be easily connected with the projector. Images can be displayed on the whiteboard and with the help of finger or any tool, there can be interaction with the images shared on the whiteboard. Interactivity, motivation, engagement and high visual representation capabilities are the main advantages of interactive white board [4].

3.2 Digital applications in education sector

Increase in the usage of ICT tools has also led to the development and usage of many digital applications in education. Some of the applications used in the online teaching-learning process are Zoom, Google meet, etc. Some of the educational institutions have developed their own customized Learning Management System (LMS) to enhance and update their teaching-learning process [5].

Along with using digital applications for teaching-learning process, various meetings including parent-teacher meetings are also being organized using the digital applications. Some of the commonly used digital applications in education are described below.

Zoom

Zoom is basically a cloud-based service that provides video conferencing option, white board, screen sharing, file sharing, etc. More updates are still ongoing to facilitate all kinds of professional sectors.
Zoom can be easily accessed with the help of smartphone, tablet, laptop and desktop. Some of the educational institutes have now started using Zoom to conduct virtual class and parent-teacher meeting.

Google Meet

This application developed by Google is an excellent video-communication service that enables the users to be connected. Teachers can easily conduct video meetings with the students to teach them the curriculum using Google Meet.

It also has features which are helpful for education. For example, along with video conferencing options, screen sharing, file sharing, etc. features are easily available for the users. In addition, attendance can also be recorded, and teachers can easily interact virtually with students in real-time. Google Meet can be easily used with the help of smartphone, tablet, laptop and desktop.

WhatsApp

WhatsApp can be used by students and teachers for sharing assignments, notes and interacting with each other. It has Group Chat feature, which is helpful for sharing assignments, notes, etc. with all the students simultaneously at one go.

Telegram

Telegram is a social messaging application whereby creating students-teachers groups, files and curriculum lecture videos can be shared with the students easily. Telegram shall be accessed with the help of smartphone, tablet, laptop and desktop.

Blogs

Nowadays, many educational blogs are written by the teachers and shared with the students. Blog also becomes a medium to interact with the students.

The use of various ICT tools as well as different digital applications for teaching and learning curriculum concepts helped, paved way and facilitated the introduction and use of AI in education sector.

To understand this better, consider the following example. As discussed and stated earlier, AI can help in education sector by conducting tests online, assessing the results as well as analyzing the results, etc. AI can also help in providing interactive learning environment and there are various other advantages of AI in education sector (which will be discussed further on) but if the ICT tools such as laptop/desktop, smartphone, etc. would not have been included in education for teaching-learning process, there would be no online test as the online test are conducted through the medium of laptop/desktop. In some cases, in the absence of laptop/desktop, students utilize smartphone or tablet for appearing for the routine online classroom test or practice test. Talking about the digital applications, if digital applications like Google Meet, etc. would have not been there, it would be difficult to have online curriculum classes.

It is because of usage of ICT tools and different digital applications in education sector that paved way for introducing something that could benefit as well as transform the education sector further and AI seemed to truly fit in for this. So, it can be rightly stated that advancements in education sector in the form of usage of ICT tools and different digital applications, facilitated the introduction and use of AI in education.

4. Advantages of AI in education for students

AI in education helps the students in learning by providing different advantages. Some of them are explained below.

Personalized learning
Online classrooms
Learning possible as per own schedule
Providing learning suggestions depending on the requirement of the students
AI based virtual assistant for answering frequently asked queries
Assistance in Curriculum development
Assisting the teachers with organizational tasks
Easing work of Administrators

4.1 Personalized learning

Personalized learning for the students is very useful. It is basically customizing learning for the students as per the need. After taking into account different factors such as which curriculum-based subjects or topics are the strengths of the student, in which particular topic or subject the students requires additional learning, etc. customization can be done, and personalized learning can be put forward.

Trying to personalize learning for each student individually will be difficult for the teachers. AI can be very helpful in this case. It can personalize learning for the students effectively. The students will benefit from personalized learning.

4.2 Online classrooms

AI tools are very efficient that they can make possible the concept of online global classrooms being accessible to the students from any part of the globe. Right now also, the students are able to learn online irrespective of their location.

AI tools are being helpful in this and students who are not able to attend classes during (Covid 19) pandemic times are still being able to learn from their homes assisted and taught by the teachers from their institutions. AI tools are part of various digital applications, platforms which are commonly used for conducting online classes. So, AI tools are facilitating the conductance of online classrooms.

Not only this but even conferences, seminars and tech talks by experts from different parts of the world are now being organized through various online platforms and knowledge dissemination is taking place throughout the globe without any hindrance and AI tools are being proving to be useful in this.

4.3 Learning possible as per own schedule

The AI based applications and tools are useful for students in learning. They provide the students with an opportunity to learn as per their will and schedule at any time.

4.4 Providing learning suggestions depending on the requirement of the students

AI in the education sector provides flexibility and easier adaptation to the requirements of the students related to the curriculum topics. AI-based application can analyze and keep track of which curriculum topic the student is searching and requires information on. The related learning materials could be then further suggested and provided to the students based on their requirement.

4.5 AI based virtual assistant for answering frequently asked queries

Teacher is an integral part of the student life. Teachers always teach the students as well as answer their queries from time to time to make their learning better. There are always some frequently asked queries in each curriculum subject. To ease out the work of the teachers, AI based virtual assistant could be helpful in answering the frequent queries of the students.

This will also benefit the students from as they can at any point of time reach out to the AI based virtual assistant and get answers to frequently asked queries.

4.6 Assistance in Curriculum development

AI could play an important role in assisting the teachers in curriculum updation/development. Based on the recent trends, cutting edge technologies and the industry needs, AI could help to update the student's curriculum.

4.7 Assisting the teachers with organizational tasks

There are various duties of a teacher other than teaching. For example, along with teaching, teachers have to complete grading of exams papers, have to prepare question papers, then there is grading of assignments, procuring lab items, preparing inventory control, mentoring, report card preparation, etc.

Teachers have to spend a lot of their time in documentation work along with teaching and class preparation work. AI is much helpful in reducing the paper work. Result Analysis, attendance details, managing the class materials through Learning Management System and lab file inventory, etc. are the tasks that can be successfully done with AI.

4.8 Easing work of administrators

Using intelligent AI based systems, the work of the administrators eases greatly. For, example, conducting and managing admissions online with the help AI based systems, eases out the work of the administrators to some extent. It can be even monitored well.

5. Concerns with AI in Education

AI does have benefits in educational sector as discussed above in the chapter, however, there are some concerns as well. To understand this better, consider the following examples.

Too much screen time
Poor face-to-face interaction
Generates need to ensure effective data management, security and data privacy

5.1 Too much screen time

AI tools help in teaching-learning process but during this process students as well as teachers have to spend their lot of time in front of the screen either of desktop, laptop, tablet or cell phone and spending too much time in front of the screen is not good.

5.2 Poor face-to-face interaction

AI tools do help in providing an interactive learning environment while studying online but there is lack of face-to-face interaction between students and teachers.

This virtual environment and non-availability of the usual classroom environment with face-to-face interaction is worrisome. It may also affect the overall study performance of the students.

5.3 Generates need to ensure effective data management, security and data privacy

Having AI based tools and systems in educational sector has advantages but at the same time it generates need to ensure that there is effective data management, and all the data remains secure and mostly importantly data privacy is maintained.

6. Discussion regarding advantages and concerns with AI in education sector

AI in education sector has advantages and some concerns as well. There will be always scope for improvement and progress. The concerns should be worked upon to find appropriate solution for it. Talking about the advantages, education sector seems to benefit with the use of AI. For example, the advantages like having personalized learning, being able to learn from any place at any time, opportunities of having global classrooms, etc. that have been observed and discussed for the education sector with the introduction and usage of AI are commendable.

All these advantages along with various other advantages of AI in education sector discussed in this chapter indicate that AI in education sector will be helpful and can transform the education sector. In fact, it is already transforming the education sector with its introduction and usage in education sector. There are some concerns regarding AI in education sector as discussed above but if they are addressed well and worked upon to find some solution for it then this will be very beneficial.

7. Conclusion

The introduction of AI is transforming the functioning of education sector. AI tools are making it easy for the students to continue with their learning from any location. AI in education sector not only helps the students but it also assists and helps the teachers and administrators in their work.

There are various advantages that AI can provide in education sector which are briefly discussed in the chapter. However, AI in education sector brings forward some concerns as well which should be worked upon, and solution should be found for it. In future, the role of AI in educational could increase further if it continues to help and benefit the students and teachers in the education sector.

References

1. De Brabander, C. J., & Glastra, F. J. (2021). The unified model of task-specific motivation and teachers' motivation to learn about teaching and learning supportive modes of ICT use. Education and Information Technologies, 26(1), 393-420.
2. Del Carmen Ramírez-Rueda, M., Cózar-Gutiérrez, R., Colmenero, M. J. R., & González-Calero, J. A. (2021). Towards a coordinated vision of ICT in education: A comparative analysis of Preschool and Primary Education teachers' and parents' perceptions. Teaching and Teacher Education, 100, 103300.
3. Teng, M. F. (2021). Interactive-whiteboard-technology-supported collaborative writing: Writing achievement, metacognitive activities, and co-regulation patterns. System, 97, 102426.
4. Tosuntaş, Ş. B., Çubukçu, Z., & Beauchamp, G. (2021). A new model for the factors that affect interactive whiteboard usage of teachers and its effect on performance. Education and Information Technologies, 1-18.
5. Rajalingam, S., Kanagamalliga, S., Karuppiah, N., & Puoza, J. C. (2021). Peer Interaction Teaching-Learning Approaches for Effective Engagement of Students in Virtual Classroom. Journal of Engineering Education Transformations, 34, 425-432.
6. Gyampoh, A. O., Ayitey, H. K., Fosu-Ayarkwah, C., Ntow, S. A., Akossah, J., Gavor, M., & Vlachopoulos, D. (2020). Tutor Perception on Personal and Institutional Preparedness for Online Teaching-Learning during the COVID-19 Crisis: The Case of Ghanaian Colleges of Education. African Educational Research Journal, 8(3), 511-518.
7. Patil, Y. M., & Kumbhar, P. D. (2021). Learning by Gamification: An Effective Active Learning Tool in Engineering Education. Journal of Engineering Education Transformations, 34, 447-453.
8. Oomen, A. (2021). Involving Students, Parents and Community in Career Development Services in Secondary Schools. The Journal for Specialists in Group Work, 1-16.
9. Bokayev, B., Torebekova, Z., Davletbayeva, Z., & Zhakypova, F. (2021). Distance learning in Kazakhstan: estimating parents' satisfaction of educational quality during the coronavirus. Technology, Pedagogy and Education, 1-13.
10. ElSaheli-Elhage, R. (2021). Access to students and parents and levels of preparedness of educators during the COVID-19 emergency transition to e-learning. International Journal on Studies in Education, 3(2), 61-69.

2

Effects of Artificial Intelligence in Education Sector

Mahalaxmi Mohan

Dept of Pharmacology, MGV's Pharmacy College, India

Abstract

Education is considered a vital aspect of an individual's future career path. Education has great importance and hence education sector is considered one of the most important sectors in the society. Education sector always keeps on upgrading and progressing and thus undergoes various changes for this purpose, especially in the past few years, education sector has undergone major changes which has resulted in bringing about great flexibility in the way and mode of teaching. Interactive clever boards, projectors and smart notebooks etc. are being used to make the education system interactive. Tablets, smartphones and other electronic devices like laptop, desktop are also being used in education sector by students and teachers for communicating, conducting classes, exchanging or sharing study material, learning, etc. which proves to be very useful. This is providing great flexibility in the education sector for both, the teachers as well as the students. Among the modern changes education sector has undergone, the change of introducing the application of Artificial Intelligence (AI) in education sector can be very advantageous. In fact, application of AI in education sector can have great effects and they are already making an impact. Introducing and applying AI strategies and tools in education sector have been identified as one of the most valuable applications in this sector. This chapter explains the effects of artificial intelligence in education sector.

1. Introduction

Education has a vital importance. In the recent times education sector has changed a lot. Advancements in technological fields such as the information and communication technology (ICT) field, etc. have helped in bringing changes in the education sector. The education sector seems to co-relate with advancements in different technological fields.

Advancements in ICT field have enabled education sector to conduct classes through ICT devices like smartphone, laptop, desktop, etc. Advancements in the field of artificial intelligence (AI) seem to be next in line along ICT which can bring changes in education sector. In fact, it has great effects, and it has already started to impact education sector in a good way. AI has various advantages which will benefit education sector.

There is constant advancement and improvement in personal computers, laptops, cellphones, etc. electronic communication devices and systems. Different computing techniques with great abilities are widely being used. All this is encouraging the development and use of AI in education sector, which is proving to have tremendous effects which are helpful.

AI is enabling personalization of learning materials according to the student's necessity. This is one of the vital effects of AI in education.

2. Advantages of the use of AI in education sector

2.1 Enhanced learning experience through personalization

AI can help in providing suggestions for learning. In fact, it can help in providing enhanced learning experience for the students through personalization. Diverse AI-enabled algorithms can suggest personalized learning concepts after studying the students' information like learning preferences, learning interests, etc.

2.2 Helps in acquiring education irrespective of time and location

AI powered tools, applications and solutions are proving to be really helpful. With advancement of AI in education sector, students through AI powered tools, applications and solutions can learn their curriculum concepts from any location at any given time. Various different study-based learning platforms and applications as well as applications which forms the means through which study classes can be conducted utilize AI powered tools.

2.3 Follows the go green concept

AI based smart classroom does not generally make use of paper, pen, pencil and printouts, this is one of the great advantages of smart study classroom era to preserve nature and follow the go green concept.

2.4 Saves time

The AI based smart tools makes sharing of notes, presentations and other curriculum related materials very easy. Teachers and students don't have to be actually present in front of each other to share notes, presentations and other study material, thanks to AI based tools. Feedback can also be provided on the shared notes, presentations, study materials, etc. quickly and easily. This saves time of students and teachers.

2.5 Smart forums are enjoyable

It is certainly amusing to use smart interactive forums consisting of facilities for teaching and interaction with students. AI based smart forums can allow teaching any subject through discussions on forums as this will make a normal routine classroom lecture interesting, enjoyable and fun for students.

2.6 Virtual mentors

AI based systems can provide feedback to the students on their performance and can act as a virtual mentor.

3. AI and educators/teachers in schools and colleges

AI based smart systems in education sector can help in carrying out responsibilities like that of grading the test results that commonly could only be carried out by teachers. In the world of education, AI is revolutionizing schools and colleges, making educators/teachers job a lot less complicated.

AI has the capability to provide personalized learning options and offer analytics-based overall performance perception. AI is making way in education sector due to its various advantages, some of which are explained above.

Its application in education sector is set to grow but with the growth of its application in education sector, certain queries and areas of concern related to student's curriculum data management, data privacy, etc. come to the forefront for which certain policies need to be made to make sure students data is safe and secure and all the other related queries and concerns should also be well addressed so that both the students as well as the educational institutes can without any worry utilize AI based tools and applications for learning and teaching curriculum subjects.

AI helps in learning from anywhere. AI permits educators to spend more teaching time with students as it can automatically carry out some administrative responsibilities like grading of exam results, conducting analysis of overall results of students in tests in a particular subject, etc.

Educators/teachers spend hours of time grading and checking papers, preparing teaching topic plan and finishing administrative chores outside the classroom. AI based systems are growing increasingly in their capabilities. They can compare the written solution in exams with the correct solution to determine that the students accurately answered the questions asked and can thus assist teachers in checking exam papers.

AI will also impact and effect on how students can research and from where. With the use of translation tools powered by AI based machine learning, students will be able to participate in global classrooms as AI can actively translate and interpret the educational data in real-time.

The AI tools can evaluate the overall results of exams to locate gaps in student overall curriculum performance. This will help in suggesting personalized learning content for the students. With AI, a lot of opportunities are emerging as available. AI in education is seeming to have numerous advantages in education not only in teaching and learning but also in carrying out administrative work as well. All the benefits offered by AI in education are emerging as very efficient.

From the above discussion and explanation in the chapter, the overall effects of AI in education are clear. They are discussed and explained below.

4. Overall effects of AI in education

4.1 Simplifying administrative duties

AI can either conduct or help in conducting the administrative responsibilities for teachers and educational establishments. Educators/teachers spend a large amount of time on grading exams, assessing homework, and giving responses to the common queries of the students. AI can now conduct and help in the grading obligations where multiple assessments are concerned which means teachers would have more time left with them which they could utilize in teaching.

Based on results, teachers can also analyze and examine students' curriculum development using the AI tools. Additionally, AI can point the areas in which that require further attention. For example, AI based tools could point out the subjects that maximum students struggled with.

AI tools can help in admission process. Admission work is time occupying work. AI can easily help in this work and thus save time and make the work easier for the teachers and other administrative staff carrying out the admission work.

4.2 Smart content

In recent times, the role of AI in education is seeming to increase. Smart content for studying can be made available using AI. Smart content basically includes virtual content like video lectures, video conferencing lectures containing explanation of curriculum topics using animation and graphics, etc.

With AI, textbooks can also take a brand-new turn. AI structures can be used in creating syllabus and customized textbooks for certain topics. Now a days, textbooks are being digitized. AI can help in making textbook contents more comprehensible and easy to navigate.

4.3 Extended help and opportunities through AI

AI has various abilities, and it can help in managing different administrative task of teachers allowing them to have increased time left with the teachers which they could utilize for teaching and carrying out other duties. Routine tasks, which include attendance could be managed with AI tools. Altogether, AI can provide extended help to teachers in their work.

AI can also provide opportunities for students in education sector. AI tools can help in real-time translation of study material and can also help in correcting grammatical errors and in learning pronunciations, meaning of the word, etc.

4.4 Personalized studying

AI can carve out personalized studying suggestions for the students. Through AI-powered applications and tools, students can get customized or personalized suggestions for studying. AI can analyze the student's exam results and related information.

4.5 Breaking distance barriers

Training has no limits, and AI can help to dispose of limitations. Technology brings drastic transitions by means of facilitating and mastering any path from everywhere throughout the globe and at any time. AI-powered tools and applications equips teachers to conduct learning lectures which students can attend from any location.

With extra inventions in future, there might be a very wide range of courses held online designed for a global classroom and with the help of AI, students could study from any location.

5. Undesirable consequences of AI in education sector

5.1 Human interaction could decrease

One of most undesirable consequences of AI in education sector would be it can decrease human interaction of student and teacher in education. With availability of different AI powered tools, devices and applications, etc. students might seek help from them which could result in decrease of student-teacher interaction.

AI powered tools, devices and applications, etc. can decrease human interaction in education. AI should help teachers and students, but it should not decrease human interaction. This consequence of AI in education is highly undesirable.

5.2 Lack of emotional intelligence

Artificial intelligence powered tools, devices, applications, etc. have no feelings. In learning and studying students need emotional support from their teachers which is very helpful for them in their learning journey.
AI powered devices, tools, machines, etc., are emotionless and have no emotional intelligence. They cannot provide the students any emotional support.

5.3 Artificial intelligence dependency

AI could create dependency on it for the work it is easing out. The aim of including AI and taking help of AI based tools in education section is basically to ease out the work, help students and teachers but getting dependent on AI is of the undesirable consequence which should be avoided from occurring.

6. Conclusion

Artificial Intelligence effects truly impacts the education sector in a huge way. There are both advantages and undesirable consequences of using AI in education. Even though in comparison, the number of undesirable consequences of using AI in education are less and the advantages are more, the solutions for overcoming the undesirable consequences should be found and worked on correctly.

With a view to gain from AI and avoid undesirable consequences of its utilization in education sector, certain guidelines or protocols must be made before including AI tools and applications in education sector. The intention of introducing AI within the study room in education sector is and always should be to ease out the work and to make the jobs of teachers less complicated and to help and benefit the students.

7. References

1. Popenici, S., and Kerr, S. Exploring the impact of artificial intelligence on teaching and learning in higher education. Research and Practice in Technology Enhanced Learning. (2017), 12: 22.
2. Lazarus, SS, Thurlow, ML, Lail, KE, Christensen, L. A longitudinal analysis of state accommodations policies: twelve years of change, 1993-2005. The Journal of Special Education. (2008) 43(2): 67-80.
3. Bayne, S. Teacherbot: interventions in automated teaching. Teaching in Higher Education. (2015), 20(4).
4. Botrel, L, Holz, EM, Kübler, A. Brain painting V2: evaluation of P300-based brain-computer interface for creative expression by an end-user following the user-centered design. Brain-Computer Interfaces. (2015) 2(2–3):1–15.
5. Chen, X, Wang, Y, Nakanishi, M, Gao, X, Jung, TP, Gao, S. High-speed spelling with a noninvasive brain–computer interface. Proceedings of the National Academy of Sciences. (2015): 112(44), E6058–E6067.
6. González, VM, Robbes, R, Góngora, G, Medina, S (2015). Measuring concentration while programming with low-cost BCI devices: differences between debugging and creativity tasks. In Foundations of augmented cognition, (pp. 605–615). Los Angeles, CA: Springer International Publishing.
7. Maderer, J. (2016). Artificial intelligence course creates AI teaching assistant. Georgia Tech News Center, 9 May 2016.
8. Lijia Chen, Pingping Chen and Zhijian Lin. Artificial Intelligence in Education: A Review, IEEE Access.2020, 8:75263-75291.
9. M. Chassignol, A. Khoroshavin, A. Klimova, and A. Bilyatdinova, "Artificial intelligence trends in education: A narrative overview," Procedia Comput. Sci., vol. 136, pp. 16–24, Jan. 2018.
10. Hu. J, Shen.L, and Sun.G, "Squeeze-and-excitation networks," in Proc. Conf. Comput. Vis. Pattern Recognit. (CVPR), 2018, pp. 7132–7141.
11. United Nations Education Scientific and Cultural Organi- zation (UNESCO). How Can Artificial Intelligence Enhance Education? [Online]. 2019 Available: https://en.unesco.org/news/how-can-artificial- intelligence-enhance-education.
12. Jake B, Christine H, Saurabh S, and Dilip W. How artificial intelligence will impact K-12 teachers. January 14, 2020, www.Mackinsey.com.
13. T. K. Wu, Y. R. Meng and S. C. Huang, Application of Artificial Neural Network to the Identification of Students with Learning Disabilities, International Conference on Arti- ficial Intelligence, 2006:162–168.
14. J. M. Fletcher, W. Coulter, D. J. Reschly and S. Vaughn, Alternative approach to the definition and identification of learning disabilities: some questions and answers, Annals of dyslexia, 54(2), 2004: 304–331.

15. V. C. Georgopoulos, G. A. Malandraki, C. D. Stylios, A fuzzy cognitive map approach to differential diagnosis of specific language impairment. Artificial Intelligence in Med- icine, 2003, 29: 261–278.
16. O. A. Schipor, S. G. Pentiuc and M. D. Schipor, Improving computer based speech therapy using a fuzzy expert system. Computing and Informatics, 2003, 22: 1001–1016.
17. J. Pavlopoulos, J. Vrettaros, G. Vouros and A. S. Drigas, The Development of a Self-Assessment system for the Learners Answers with the Use of GPNN. WSKS, 2008, 1: 332–340.
18. I. Rapin and R. F. Tuchman, Autism: Definition, neurobiology, screening, diagnosis. Pediatric Clinics of North America, 2008, 55(5):1129–1146.
19. M. Riedl, R. Arriaga, F. Boujarwah, H. Hong, J. Isbell and L. J. Heflin, Graphical Social Scenarios: Toward Intervention and Authoring for Adolescents with High Functioning Autism, Virtual Healthcare Interaction, Papers from the AAAI Fall Symposium, 2007.
20. B. M. Macmillan, Rhyme and reading: A critical review of the research methodology, Journal of Research in Reading, 2002, 25(1): 4–42.
21. L. Roberts and S. McDougall, Explaining Performance in the Orthographic Analogy Task: Phonological Priming, Phonological Skills and Letter-sound Knowledge. Journal of Experimental Child Psychology, 2003, 84(4): 310–337.
22. K. Jain, P. Manghirmalani, J. Dongardive and S. Abraham, Computational Diagnosis of Learning Disability, International Journal of Recent Trends in Engineering,2009, 2(3).
23. M. Kohli and T. V. Prasad, Identifying Dyslexic Students by Using Artificial Neural Networks, Proceedings of the World Congress on Engineering, London, U.K., 1, 2010.2
24. E. Melis, E. Andres, J. Budenbender, A. Frischauf, G.Goguadze, P. Libbrecht, M. Pollet and C. Ullrich, ACTI- VEMATH, A Generic and Adaptive Web-Based Learning Environment, International Journal of Artificial Intelligence, 2001, 24(4):1–25.
25. N. Livne, L. Nava, O. Livne and C. Wight, Can automated scoring surpass hand grading of students' constructed responses and error patterns in mathematics? MERLOT Journal of Online Learning and Teaching, 2007, 3(3).
26. G. Rebolledo-Mendez and S. De Freitas, Attention modeling using inputs from a Brain Computer Interface and user-generated data in Second Life. In: The Tenth International Conference on Multimodal Interfaces (ICMI 2008), Crete, Greece, 2008.

3

Intelligent Student Companion

Prakash, J. and Shyam Ganesh, C.R.

PSG College of Technology, Coimbatore, India

Abstract

The education sector has undergone various changes especially with the presence and application of Information and Communication Technology (ICT) tools which are used widely in education. Despite the changes and irrespective of the mode of the education, whether it is online or offline mode, one thing doesn't change is the tendency of the students to list down and take note of certain points of curriculum topic which they are being taught. This is actually very helpful as the listed and noted points by the students are like a short summary of the topic or act like a short summary of the topic and help them in remembering and revising the curriculum topic. However, there is one common difficulty which arises here, i.e., when classes are conducted continuously back-to-back for a longer period of time, it becomes little difficult sometimes for the students to list out and take note of certain points of the curriculum topic that is being taught in the class. To help the students, a system named Intelligent Student Companion (ISC) which can automatically take note and present summary-based points or in other words summary content of the curriculum topic which is being taught in the class and present it to the students at any point of time is suggested. ISC system in simple words is an application (app) which requires the audio file of the curriculum classes to be uploaded and fed to it as input. So, the audio file of what the teacher is teaching in the class needs to be uploaded. The app will then with the help of text-to-speech API, neural network and other elements, provide notes in summary form to the students. These summary-based notes will be stored in the app and the students will be able to view it any point of time. This suggested app can replace the existing way in which notes are handwritten by students during curriculum classes. This chapter suggests and explains ISC app for digitizing and automating the process of taking notes and managing them, which will make students' work easier. ISC can actually serve as an assistant to a student by taking notes consisting of the summary of the curriculum topics being taught for every lecture and managing it.

1. Introduction

Sometimes, it is difficult for the students to write down the summary of the particular curriculum topic which is being taught in the class. The Intelligent Student Companion (ISC) can be very helpful in such situations. The ISC application is that which intakes recorded audio file of teacher's lectures and converts it into text utilising the Google Speech-to-Text API.

The text file produced is cleaned and processed to find keywords and to generate a summary of the topic taught and is stored in an organised database. It will help students greatly as at the end product of suggested ISC, students can view the summary notes according to the subject by initial login in this ISC android application.

ISC can replace the existing system in which notes are handwritten and at times little tough to manage, thus digitizing and automating the process and making students' work easier. ISC can truly serve as an assistant to a student by generating summary notes of the curriculum topic taught in the class lecture and can very well manage and maintain the notes automatically.

The system working can be understood in different steps. Firstly, the recorded audio which is uploaded in this app is pushed to the database where it is stored as Mp3 file. This mp3 file is then processed with the voice to text feature and gets a text file as output. The backend database used for the ISC app is Firebase.

After this, the text file gets processed using a python script and then it is stored in the database. Finally, the students can fetch the text notes from the database using the android application. The android application was the chosen mode of deployment as it makes it easier to be utilized.

ISC enables smart and hassle-free maintenance of notes subject wise which not only eases students' work but also saves time. ISC can reformulate the workflow of students in classroom. Notes are stored in database, which is powered by the cloud storage, enabling students to access it at anytime from anywhere.

2. Neural network language model for ISC

For developing the ISC, neural network language was required. A language model can predict the probability of the next word in the sequence, based on the words already observed in the sequence.

Neural network models are a preferred method for developing statistical language models because they can use a distributed representation where different words with similar meanings have similar representation. They can also use a large context of recently observed words when making predictions.

The neural network language model has a few unique characteristics such as:

- It uses a distributed representation for words so that different words with similar meanings will have a similar representation.
- It learns the representation at the same time as learning the model.
- It learns to predict the probability for the next word using the context of the last 100 words.

For developing ISC, an embedding layer is used to learn the representation of words and a Long Short-Term Memory (LSTM) recurrent neural network to learn to predict words based on their context.
One can define and fit the language model on the training data. The learned embedding needs to know the size of the vocabulary and the length of input sequences.

It also has a parameter to specify how many dimensions will be used to represent each word which is basically the size of the embedding vector space.

A dense fully connected layer with 100 neurons connects to the LSTM hidden layers to interpret the features extracted from the sequence. The output layer predicts the next word as a single vector the size of the vocabulary with a probability for each word in the vocabulary.

A SoftMax activation function is also used to ensure the outputs have the characteristics of normalized probabilities. This is an important process in development of ISC.

3. System setup for ISC

For the system setup for ISC, the android device should have a memory of 3 GB or higher, running with android marshmallow or higher version. ISC requires python 3.x with libraries such as TensorFlow, keras and google-cloud-admin is also required to be installed.

It uses Rapid Keyword Extraction algorithm (RAKE) for extracting keywords and Seq2Seq encoder-decoder model for abstractive text summarization with word representation using GloVe which is an algorithm that is used for distributed word representation. The mobile app development was done using Android studio (Java).

4. ISC system design

The system consists of three parts as it can be seen in Fig. 1. First, the recorded audio file is uploaded to upload audio part. Then the audio converts to text, does the processing and summarization of the text and finally saves it to the database.

The database is responsible for storing the summary-based notes. ISC fetches the notes from database according to the option of notes selected to be viewed by the student and displays them. The overall design of the ISC system is shown in Fig. 1.

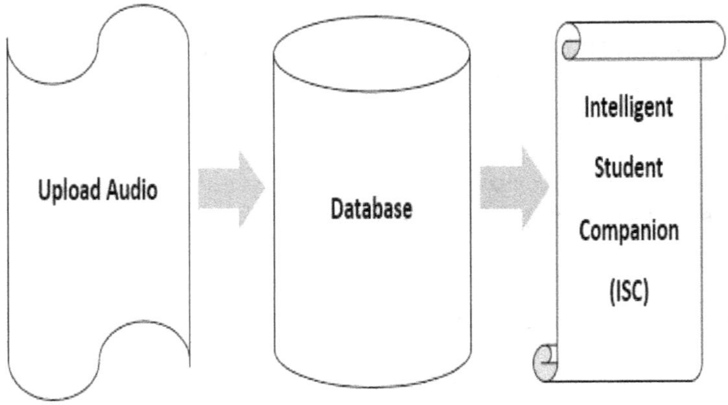

Fig. 1: Overall system design of ISC.

At the Server end, the recorded audio of the handled class is uploaded after the class ends, the recorded audio is converted into text. The transcribed text is given to keyword extraction algorithm and neural network to generate keywords and summary which is stored in the database. The design model of server module is shown in Fig. 2.

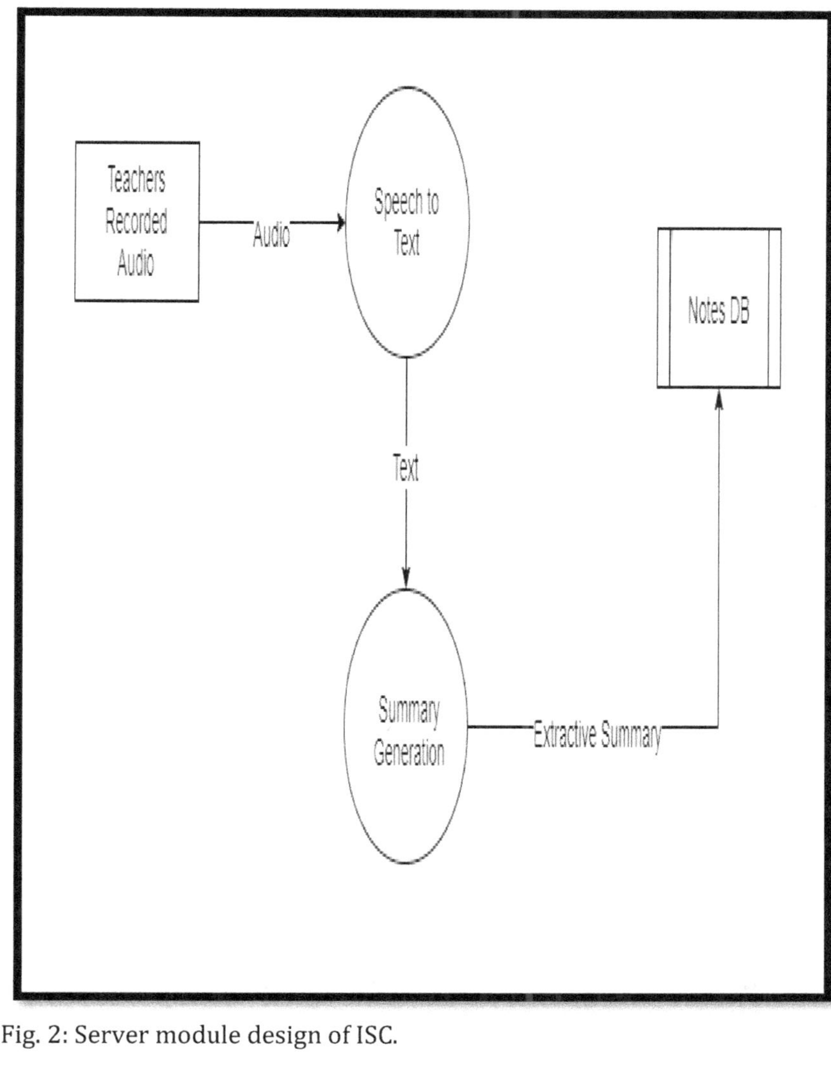

Fig. 2: Server module design of ISC.

In the mobile app, the student can login by giving his/her credentials such as an email ID. Then, the user can view the notes after it is fetched from the database. The workflow design of Student Application module is shown in Fig. 3.

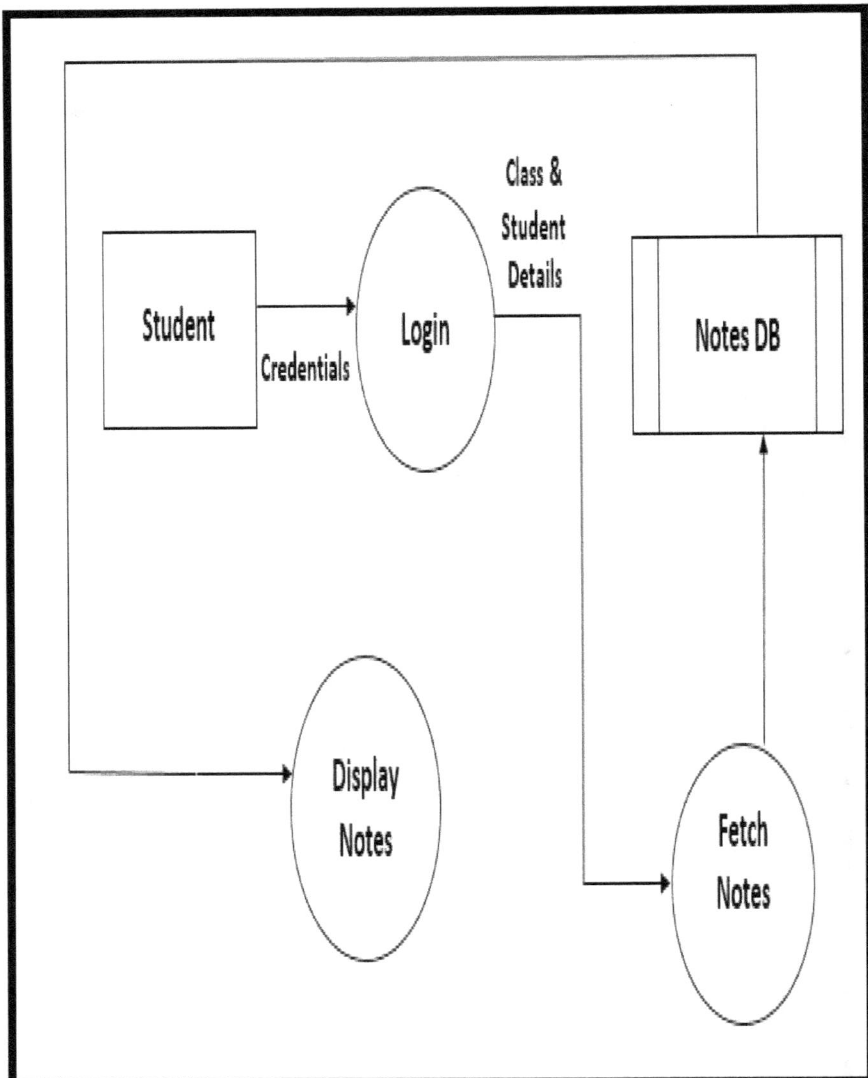

Fig. 3: Mobile application module design of ISC.

5. Intelligent student companion modules

The ISC system will be implemented as Teacher and Student module. With teacher module, one can access the features like Home, Uploading Audio and Text Summarization.

The Student module have different features which are as follows:

- Login
- Signup
- Home page
- All Notes
- Class Mode
- Display Notes

There will be a separate home page for teacher's and students' modules. The detailed description of each feature is described below.

5.1 Login as student

A user is anyone who is a student. The user shall be allowed to view the notes that have been stored in the database.

A user will be allowed login into ISC app by giving the login credentials. Those login credentials are:

- A valid email ID
- Password

The registered users can login using their email id and password. So only these two things are required for logging in the intelligent student companion.

The login method is kept simple yet secure. Through this method of login, the registered users' credentials can be verified with the credentials already stored in the database, thus making sure of authenticated login.

If the user is a first-time user, he/she can sign up using the option given below. The layout of login module of mobile application is shown in Fig. 4.

Fig. 4: Login module of ISC.

5.2 Signup

The layout of registration module of mobile application is shown in Fig. 5.

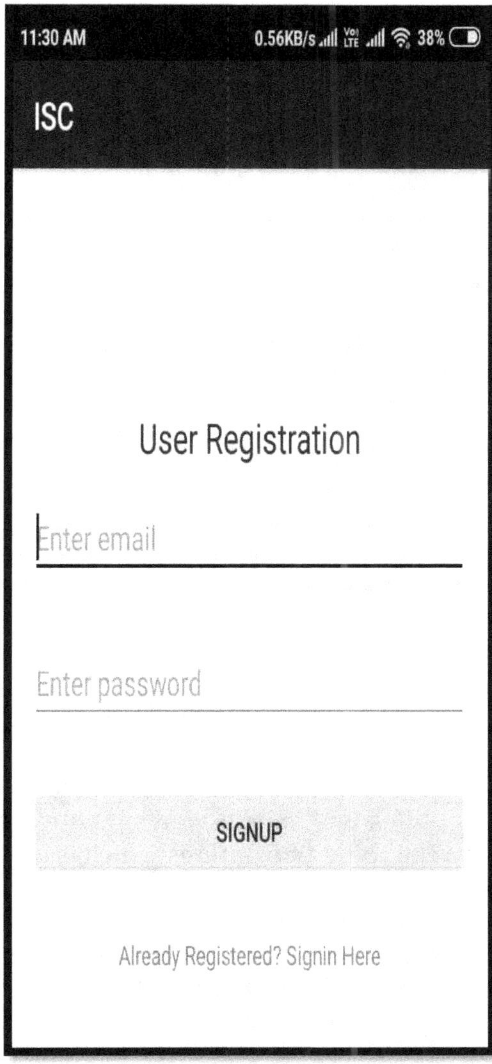

Fig. 5: Registration module of ISC.

The first-time users are required to create an account. This can be done by providing a valid email address and password.

A new user using the ISC will be redirected to signup module by selecting the option of signup here.

The user shall also be redirected to signup page if the username entered is invalid. In a signup page the user should fill in his/her details of e-mail id and password.

The e-mail id and password will be validated for redundancy once the signup button is clicked, and the details will be updated in the database. Eventually the user will be logged-in to the ISC app.

5.3 ISC Home page

The user will be allowed to view the ISC home page only on a successful login or signup.

The homepage of ISC is carefully designed with only the required options being placed in this homepage.

The user will be shown the menu to select a mode. The home page contains three options which are:

- View notes
- Class mode
- Logout

The two options, class mode and view notes will help in viewing notes. Both these options will help in viewing notes, and the prevalent difference between these two options which is explained further on in the chapter.

The logout option will be redirected to the login module. All the three options are having different functionalities. All three options work according to their designated functionalities.

The layout of ISC Home Page of mobile application is shown in Fig. 6.

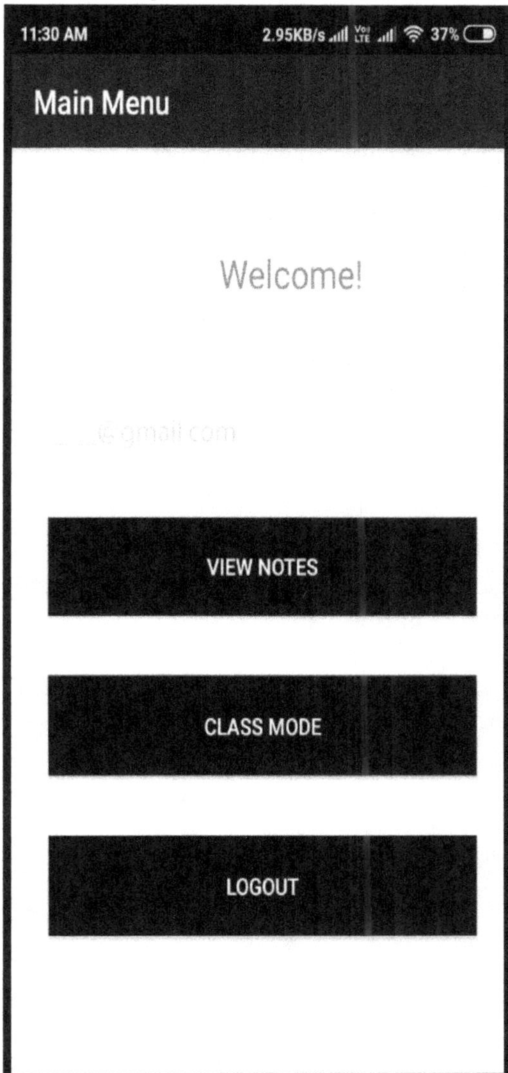

Fig. 6: Homepage module of ISC.

5.4 Class mode

In this mode, the user is presented with list of subjects available from which the student can choose the subject which he/she wants. This will open the notes of the last class of that subject.

The class notes will be retrieved from the database where it is stored. The layout of ISC Class Mode page of mobile application is shown in Fig. 7.

If student wants to read the notes of the last class of a particular subject, then they can read it through class mode. This mode will help the students in getting to read the notes of the last class of any particular subject.

The class mode makes it easier for students to go through notes.
In the below Fig. 7, different subjects are represented as

- 15z601
- 15z603
- 15z604
- 15z017

Here for example purpose they are denoted as 15z601, 15z603, etc. but the actual subject names can be stated.

Hence, the class mode is very carefully designed, and it is helpful for students to go through notes using class mode.

Fig. 7: Class module of ISC.

5.5 View notes

This mode will allow the user to view all the notes of a particular subject. Unlike class mode where notes of only the last class can be read by selecting any subject, view notes allows all the notes of any selected subject to be read by the user.

This option displays all the notes from latest to old. The user gets only the preview of all the notes initially when the user selects any particular subject.

Then by clicking and selecting on any note, he/she is redirected to view the entire note. Thus, from view notes option, the notes can be easily read by the user for studying.
This view notes option is well designed to help students.

5.6 Homepage of teacher's module

This module is used to upload the audio as teacher completes taking the lesson. The recorded audio is stored in file.

Then, with this file with the help of Google API, the audio is converted to text. These texts are stored in a database.

Summarization is also done here from the text obtained. The layout of ISC Teacher Module page of mobile application is shown in Fig. 8.

Fig. 8: Teacher module of ISC.

5.7 Uploading audio

This module allows the teacher to upload the recorded audio to the Google cloud. Hence this can be then used to convert to text. The upload module layout of ISC mobile application is shown in Fig. 9.

Fig. 9: Upload audio module of intelligent student companion.

5.8 Summarization

The sample summarization of the recording is shown in Fig. 10.

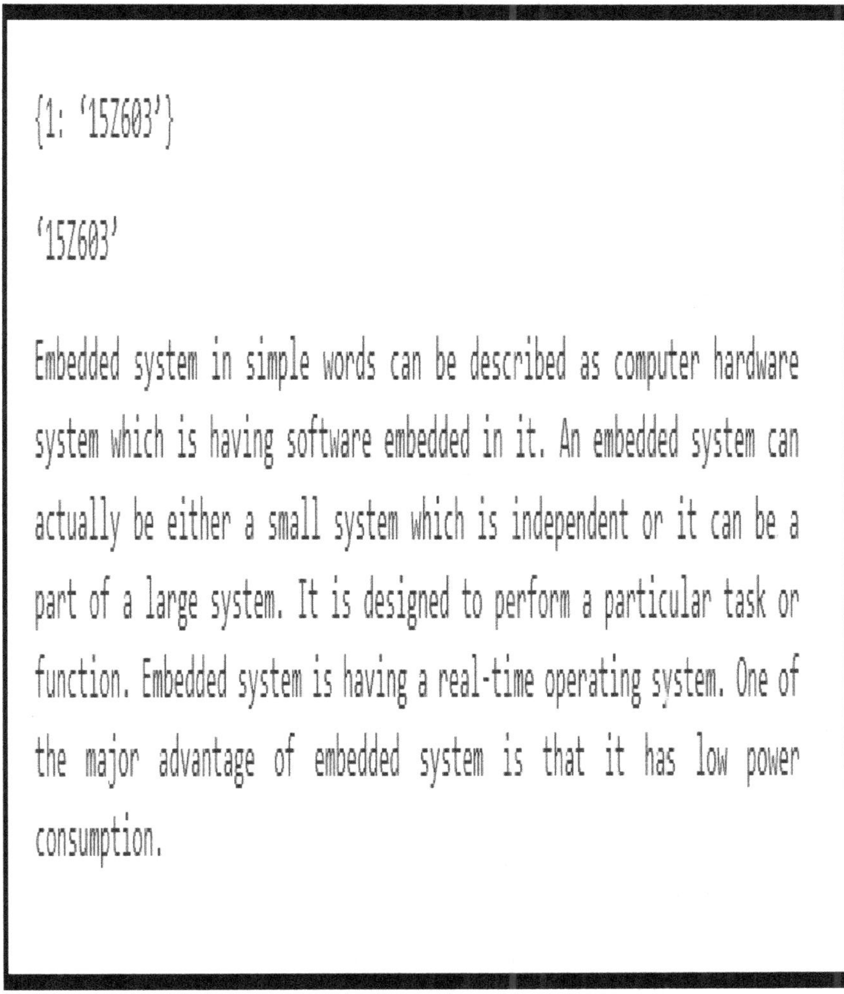
{1: '15Z603'}

'15Z603'

Embedded system in simple words can be described as computer hardware system which is having software embedded in it. An embedded system can actually be either a small system which is independent or it can be a part of a large system. It is designed to perform a particular task or function. Embedded system is having a real-time operating system. One of the major advantage of embedded system is that it has low power consumption.

Fig. 10: Summarized output.

This module is used to prepare summarized notes of the class with the help of text-to-speech API, neural network and other elements using the audio files that is uploaded.

Then a summarization is created, and this is uploaded to the database. Fig. 10 is showing one sample summarization generated and stored in database.

6. Future Scope of Developments for ISC

The only concern regarding ISC is that the notes could have some errors if there is inaccuracy in the voice to text translation and the keyword prediction models.

So, in future scope developments for ISC, it needs to make sure that voice to text translation have complete accuracy.
Along with this, the future development of the application shall include timetable integration, bandwidth usage and predictive suggestions.

7. Conclusion

In this chapter Intelligent Student Companion application is introduced, explained and suggested for students for taking notes in class. This app could prove to be very helpful for the students.
It will not only make their work easier but also save their time. It is also great option for handling and managing the notes in a hassle free manner.

References

1. Deepali K. Gaikwad, and C. Namrata Mahender, (2016) "A Review Paper on Text Summarization," *International Journal of Advanced Research in Computer and Communication Engineering*, 5(5).
2. Regina Barzilay and Michael Elhadad. (1999) "Using Lexical Chains for Text Summarization".
3. Joel Larocca Neto, Celso A. A. Kaestner and Alex A. Freitas. (2002) "Automatic Text Summarization Using A Machine Learning Approach".
4. Daniel Jurafsky and James H.Martin. (2008) "Speech and Language Processing" *Pearson*.
5. R. Mihalcea, and P. Tarau. (2004) "Textrank: Bringing Order into Texts,". *Conference on Empirical Methods in Natural Language Processing*.
6. G. Erkan, and D. R. Radev. (2004) "Lexrank: Graph-Based Lexical Centrality as Salience in Text Summarization,". *Journal of Artificial Intelligence Research*, 22(1), 457-479.

7. J. Jagadeesh, P. Pingali, and V. Varma. (2005) "Sentence Extraction Based Single Document Summarization", *Workshop on Document Summarization.*
8. R. Nallapati, B. Zhou, C. dos Santos, C. Gulcehre, and B. Xiang. (2016) "Abstractive Text Summarization Using Sequence-to-Sequence RNNs And Beyond,". *In Computational Natural Language Learning.*
9. S. Jean, K. Cho, R. Memisevic, and Yoshua Bengio. (2014) "On Using Very Large Target Vocabulary for Neural Machine Translation", *CoRR*, abs/1412.2007.

4

Effect of Introducing Cloud Computing in the Education Sector

V. Malathi[a] and V. Kavitha[b]

[a]*Department of Information Technology, SNMV College of Arts and Science, Coimbatore, Tamilnadu, India*
[b]*PG and Research Department of Computer Applications, Hindustan College of Arts and Science, Coimbatore, India*

Abstract

Education is a vital factor for development. Educational institutes keep on searching for technology which can help them. Cloud computing is one such evolving technology that can highly benefit different organizations like educational institutes, etc. with its great working capabilities. In this chapter, a brief introduction of cloud computing is given. Along with it, how cloud computing can be useful for education sector is discussed and its effects in education sector are examined and stated.

1. Introduction

Cloud computing has impacted various sectors with its presence. Generally, cloud computing is considered to impact the business sector but off lately it is impacting various sectors including education sector. Cloud computing currently is utilized in many sectors.

The main reason behind its growth and utilization in different sectors is the benefits which it provides to its users. Cloud computing's big benefits are that it is cost-effective, and productivity of its services is remarkable. These are just two big advantages of cloud computing. There are various more benefits of cloud computing which will discussed later on in the chapter in detail.

With various benefits to offer to the users, the cloud is a wellspring of usefulness for the users. It is something which can prove to be beneficial for the users.

In education sector, different educational institutions in establishment are working using the cloud to build availability and connectivity of resources and data. This is a progressive approach from the times of a storing data in floppy disk and stockpiling it.

Cloud computing is efficient. Moreover, the entire education sector can highly benefit by the utilization of cloud computing. It has the ability to help the educational sector in different ways which will be discussed later on in the chapter.

Cloud computing is helpful not only in the educational sector but also in many other sectors as it has different advantages, hence it is used in many other sectors along with the educational sector.

2. Cloud computing

Cloud computing is basically providing on-request resources like data storage, computing, etc. to the user over the Internet. Rather than purchasing, processing, and keeping up actual servers and data centers, one can easily get benefits of cloud computing. Some of the examples of the cloud service providers are as follows:

- Google Cloud
- Amazon Web Services (AWS)
- Microsoft Azure
- Salesforce
- Oracle
- IBM Cloud, etc.

2.1 Cloud computing service models

All the cloud computing service models have different set of services. Figure 1 below shows different cloud computing service models.

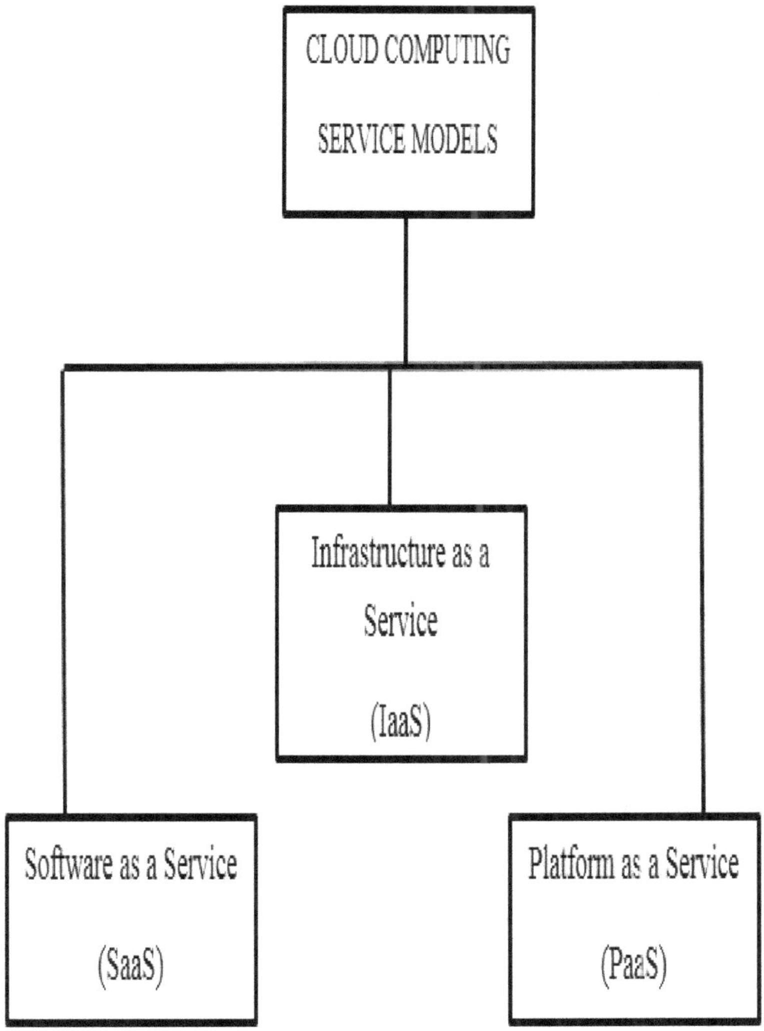

Figure 1. Cloud computing service models.

As seen in Figure 1 above, there are three cloud computing service models which are

- SaaS (Software as a Service)

- IaaS (Infrastructure as a Service)
- PaaS (Platform as a Service)

Each of the cloud computing service models are explained below.

Software as a Service (SaaS)

Software as a Service is a model that provides access to software-based applications to be utilized as a service. The service can be availed via internet.

Without having the software situated in their systems, the users can easily utilize all the benefits and applications of the software through the internet as a service.

Infrastructure as a Service (IaaS)

Infrastructure as a Service is an arrangement of infrastructure related resources like that of computing, storage, etc. in a virtual manner. Organizations or any end user can gain access and benefit from the infrastructure related resources through IaaS cloud service model.

Organizations can select this cloud service model as per the necessity of their organization without the need to actually build infrastructure at their places.

Platform as a Service (PaaS)

Platform as a Service is a cloud-based model which provides users with facilities to develop, build and run different applications. It receives the required resources through the internet as a service without having to actually build the hardware infrastructure.

Table 1. Example of SaaS, IaaS and PaaS cloud computing models

Cloud Computing Service Models	**Examples**
SaaS	Google G Suite, Microsoft Office 365, Dropbox, etc.
IaaS	Amazon Web Services, Microsoft Azure, Google Compute Engine, etc.
PaaS	Google App Engine, AWS Elastic Beanstalk, etc.

2.2 Cloud deployment model

There are different types of cloud deployment models. They are as follows:

- Public cloud
- Private cloud
- Hybrid cloud
- Community cloud

Public cloud

As the name recommends, this kind of cloud deployment model backs all clients who need to utilize resources like CPU, storage, server, database, etc. by providing them resources through internet on a membership basis or either free of cost of or pay as per usage basis.

All the resources, i.e., hardware and software resources in public cloud are shared by institutions, organizations, etc. utilizing them. Each institution, organization, etc. whoever is utilizing the public cloud can easily avail the resources through internet as mentioned above.

Private cloud

In accordance with its name, in a private cloud there is no sharing of resources, and they are utilized privately by a single institution or organization unlike public cloud where resources are shared. Private clouds are very secure and ensure the safekeeping of the data.

Hybrid cloud

A hybrid cloud is a cloud deployment model which utilizes a combination of a multi cloud which includes at least a single private and at least a single public cloud where services and applications are orchestrated between them.

Community cloud

Community cloud is the cloud infrastructure that is allowing specific set of organizations to utilize services. These organizations have similar kind of cloud service-related requirements. In other words, community cloud means cloud infrastructure where a specific set of organizations within a community which are having similar kind of cloud service-related requirements are allowed to utilize services.

3. Benefits of cloud computing

Below are some benefits of cloud computing which are the major reasons that institutions and organizations are moving to cloud computing technology-based services:

- Budget Savings
- Strategic edge
- Quick availability and access
- Safe back-up of data
- Dependability

As it can be seen benefits like budget savings, strategic edge, quick availability and access, etc. are provided by cloud computing. All the benefits are discussed below.

Budget savings: It provides generous saving in capital expense as users can avail all the required cloud computing services without any investment for building and maintaining physical hardware setup. The enterprises have to only pay for the cloud computing services they require and till the time they are utilizing the services which ultimately results into budget savings.

Strategic edge: It enables users to avail the most recent features applications related to the cloud computing services at any time.

Quick availability and access: The cloud computing services can be availed quickly and can be accessed easily from anywhere.

Safe back-up of data: When users are utilizing cloud-based services, there is a safe back-up of data provided.

Dependability: Dependability is one of the greatest benefits of cloud computing

4. Cloud computing in the education sector

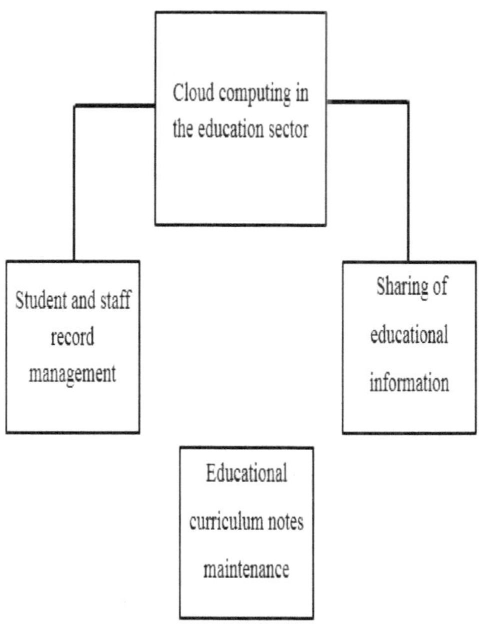

Figure 2. Examples of some uses of cloud computing in education.

- Student and staff record management
- Educational curriculum notes maintenance
- Distribution of educational information

Student and staff record management: The records of both, students and staff can be put up at cloud and can be saved there. Management of the records will become much easier by saving the records at cloud as any staff member or administrative member can access the records whenever required and can update them.

Educational curriculum notes maintenance: The teachers can store and save educational curriculum notes at cloud. All the notes can be maintained at cloud and the teachers can keep on updating them as per the requirement. The students can access it from anywhere.

Sharing of educational information: Any educational information can be saved at cloud and easily shared among students, staff members or administrative members.

The education institutes can thus benefit from implementation of cloud computing. In schools and universities, educators, learners, administration staff can set up their records and store them on cloud as explained above.

Educational institutes can store not only the profiles of instructors, in fact they can allocate the classes for them and store and share this information and other required information among the staff through cloud. They can even have timetable schedules stored on cloud.

Along with this, the concerns of carrying around delicate CD-ROMs for accessing or obtaining the stored information seem to have disappeared with the emergence of cloud computing.

The educational sector is exploring this compelling and productive space-saving innovation. Cloud computing is protected, steady, and amazingly simple to utilize innovation.

5. The impact of cloud computing on education

Cloud computing is impacting a number of different areas, including education. It has the ability to help benefit the education sector. Data can be easily stored and kept secure using cloud computing. All the data can be shared among staff and students of an educational institute with great ease from any location through cloud.

From educational notes to important documents, everything can be stored and shared easily. The stored data at the cloud can accessed from any location like mentioned above and can thus reach to the person(s) to whom the data needs to be sent at any location.

Cloud computing is also easy to work with and efficient and altogether it makes the work easier. This way with all the different benefits cloud computing provides as discussed above, it has an overall great impact on cloud computing.

6. Benefits of cloud computing in education

There are various benefits of cloud computing, and the cloud is a valuable asset. The benefits of cloud computing in education are discussed and described below.

Better Portability

Previously for transferring and storing data, CD drives, USB drives, etc. were used and were required to be taken from one place to another whenever needed.
Presently, with the appearance of cloud computing, there is no compelling reason to stress over porting stockpiling CD or any gadgets around. The teachers can get all the data required from the cloud without the need to carry any additional CD or gadgets.

Access Anywhere, Anytime

Daily work schedule, notes, any required document resources all can be put up and saved at cloud from anywhere and at any time. The teachers or students can effectively download the required data or add any data or simply just access the data whenever they want from any spot.

Safety and Security of data

Cloud computing provides safety and security of data. The uploaded data remains secure and safely stored at cloud.

Collaborate and Share

From time to time, all the necessary notes or documents can be collaborated and shared among the students and staff easily from any location through the cloud.

Ease in working

Cloud computing is easy to work with and provides great ease in working. The educational institutes can according to their requirements select the cloud model and avail the cloud computing resources without actually having to build and maintain the infrastructure.

Budget Friendly

Cloud computing resources can be purchased from cloud service provider as per requirement and are budget friendly.

7. Current scenario of cloud computing in education system

Covid-19 pandemic made education shift online which increased the utilization of cloud in education sector. Nevertheless, even without the pandemic, cloud computing was being utilized to a great extent in education sector, the only change is that ever since the pandemic its utilization has increased.

Cloud computing-based innovations are one of the requested and effectively growing areas of the cutting-edge IT domain. The utilization of cloud innovations in the educational sector is thus increasing.

8. Conclusion

Today, cloud computing is of importance in an educational environment. It offers learners, instructors, and authoritative personnel great advantages of utilization of cloud computing. With the capacity to reduce IT expenditures and simultaneously establish an advanced working atmosphere, instructive organizations like the educational sector institutes often notice some significant benefits of shifting to the cloud.

The modernization of education measures and the inclusion of the most recent innovations in the education sector encourages development and progress which is one of the most essential objectives of any sector. In this respect, it is clear that the cloud is an important asset in the field of education.
As a result, it will be rewarding for educational institutions to move to the cloud road to experience useful benefits of innovation.

References

[1] Abdul Rahman, Shahzad Sarfraz, Umar Shoaib, Ghulam Abbas and Muhammad Atif Sattar (December 2016), "Cloud based E-Learning, Security Threats and Security Measures", Indian Journal of Science and Technology. Vol. 9, No. 48.
[2] Abusfian Elgelany, Weam Gaoud Alghabban (January 2017), "Cloud Computing: Empirical Studies in Higher Education A Literature Review", International Journal of Advanced Computer Science and Applications. Vol. 8, No. 10, 2017, pp 121-127.
[3] Alamri, and Qureshi (2015)," Usability of Cloud Computing to Improve Higher Education," Modern Education and Computer Science Press, vol. 9.
[4] Buyya, R. et al (2009). Cloud Computing and emerging IT platforms: Vision, Hype and reality for delivering computing as the 5th Utility. Future Generation Computer Systems.
[5] Dr. Jenny Wang (2017), "Cloud Computing Technologies In Writing Class: Factors Influencing Students" Learning Experience", Turkish Online Journal of Distance Education-TOJDE, Volume: 18 Number: 3
[6] Ercan, T. (2010), "Effective Use of Cloud Computing in Educational Institutions", Procedia Social and Behavioral Sciences, 2, 938–942.
[7] Fahad A. Alghamdi (January 2018) An Integrated Cloud model for intelligent E-Learning system. International Journal of Applied Engineering Research. Vol. 13, No. 14, pp 11484-11490.
[8] Gaurav Bhatia, Mohnish Anand, Priya Shrivastava (2012), " Cloud Computing Technology In Education System", International Journal of Advanced Technology & Engineering Research (IJATER), ISSNNO:2250-3536 Volume2, Issue2.
[9] Jolly Upadhyaya, Neelu Jyothi Ahuja, Kapil Dev Sharma (January 2019) Evaluating User Expectations and Quality of service: A Novel Approach to

Understanding Cloud Services. International Journal of Recent Technology and Engineering. Vol. 7, No. 5S2, pp 381-385.
[10] Kamal Kant Hiran, Anders Henten, Mahendra Kumar Shrivas, Ruchi Doshi (October 2018) Hybrid EduCloud Model in Higher Education: The case of Sub-Saharan Africa, Ethiopia. In proceedings of 2018 IEEE 7th International Conference on Adaptive Science & Technology (ICAST).
[11] Katz et al.(2009), "Demystifying Cloud Computing for Higher Education." ECAR Research Bulletin. Web. Sep 22.
[12] Kishan Mali, Dr. Snehlata Kothari (May 2020,) "Cloud Computing In School Education: A Study Enlightening Benefits and Challenges", International Journal of New Technology and Research (IJNTR) ISSN: 2454-4116, Volume-6, Issue-5, Pages 17-26
[13] Lakshminarayanan, Kumar and Raju (2014), "Cloud Computing Benefits for Educational Institutions", Information Security and Computer Fraud, vol. 2, no. 1, pp. 5-9.
[14] Luo, Li (2015), "The Application and Research of Information Technology of Cloud Computing in Colleges and Universities," International Conference on Materials Engineering and Information Technology Applications.
[15] Mallikharjuna Rao, N., Sasidhar, C., Satyendra Kumar, V. (2013), "Cloud Computing Through Mobile Larning", International Journal of Advanced Computer Science and Applications, Vol.1, No. 6,
[16] Maria Teresa Baldassarre, Danilo Caivano, Giovanni Dimauro, Enrica Gentile, and Giuseppe Visaggio (February 2018) Cloud Computing for Education: A Systematic Mapping Study. IEEE Transactions on Education.
[17] Mladen A. Vouk (2018)," Cloud Computing – Issues, Research and Implementations", Journal of Computing and Information Technology - CIT 16, 2008, 4, 235–246 doi:10.2498/cit.1001391
[18] Neelakantan.P (February 2018) A Study on Elearning and Cloud Computing. International Journal of Scientific Research in Computer Science, Engineering and Information Technology. Vol. 3, No. 1, pp 1534-1539.
[19] Rehana Parveen and Emna Chikhaoui(2017), "Legal Issues and Challenges in Educational Cloud Computing in the Kingdom of Saudi Arabia", International Journal of Economic Research, Vol.14, No.20, Page No.357-371.

5

Artificial Intelligence, Big Data and Cloud Computing Oriented Applications in Education Sector

Pedro Pablo Chambi Condori

Universidad Nacional Jorge Basadre Grohmann, Tacna, Peru

Abstract

This book chapter aims to discuss artificial intelligence (AI), big data and cloud computing oriented applications in education sector. The adoption of Artificial Intelligence (AI), big data and cloud computing in education has the potential to bring changes in the educational teaching-learning process. It can benefit the education sector. In this chapter, the application of AI, big data and cloud computing in education sector along with its advantages is discussed and presented.

1. Overview

Artificial intelligence abbreviated as AI has its existence dated back to many years. Its application in education can portray visible advantages. In addition to AI, application of cloud computing and big data can also portray visible advantages in education sector.

2. Introduction

AI in general is very impactful and has many effects. It has great functionalities. AI is the ability of computer systems or machines to learn and make decisions like humans. In other words, AI means the computer systems or machines can carry out tasks which need human intelligence.

Application of AI can have great effects on education sector. John McCarthy is the person who coined the term artificial intelligence in 1956. A workshop meeting named Dartmouth Summer Research Project was held at Dartmouth College and at this workshop meeting, the term Artificial Intelligence was coined. Since then, AI has evolved.

Technologies like big data and cloud computing have also evolved. The application of them in the education sector can have large effects and can result in many changes in these sectors.

3. Literature review

Described below are some papers which were reviewed by the author.

Paper title	Authors	Description of the topic studied
Artificial Intelligence Innovation in education: A twenty -year data -driven historical analysis.	Guan, C., Mou, J., Jiang, Z. (2020) [8]	In this paper, the authors have gone through and reflected on twenty years of educational research-based data. The authors retrieved 400 research articles which were on the application of AI and deep learning (DL) techniques in teaching and learning and presented it in their article. They have stated different paradigm shifts and trends observations in the educational research area which they found out from their study.
Emerging Techonologies to Smart Education	Palanivel, K. (2020) [10]	This paper addresses how different emerging technologies like the blockchain, cloud computing, big data, IoT can help in making education system intelligent. The traditional education methods are described and the difficulties occurring in them are specified. How modern emerging overcome these

		difficulties and how they can make education system smart is discussed in this paper by the author.
Smart education: A Review and Future Research Directions	Martín, A.C.; Alario-Hoyos, C.; Kloos, C.D. (2019). [1]	In this paper, the authors carry out a literature review on what is smart education, what technologies are used in it and how it works. Through this literature review, the authors discussed in the paper regarding the previous works and came to know about the role and application of different technologies in education and what developments they can make in education sector. The authors mentioned that more research needs to be carried out on this topic but through this review they got a fair idea and knowledge of what is smart education and also regarding application and role of various different technologies in education sector.
Artificial Intelligence trends in education: a narrative overview.	Chassignol, M., Khoroshavin, A. Klimova, A. [3]	The article addresses what impact AI can have on education. The authors have carried out a literature review, through which they try to state how AI can possibly reshape the education sector.

Impact of modern technology in education.	Raja, R. and Nagasubramani, P. C. [13]	In this paper, the authors have discussed regarding the impact of technology in education, analyzed and concluded that there are positive and negative impacts, among the positive impacts, they mention the enhancements in learning and teaching, also the participation of students in education from different places of the world leads to students studying together online from any place in the world, etc. Among the negative impacts, the authors mention the following aspects: the decrease in writing skills in students due to the excessive use of digital technology, lack of focus due to being connected to online world or call it virtual world, etc. The authors conclude that advantages should be taken from the positive things that technology brings in education and the negative impacts or drawbacks should be eliminated.

Table 1 Summarizes the references in relation to topics covered in various articles published between 2018 and 2020. The references shown in Table 1, comprised in the period 2018 to 2020, lists different researchers who have dealt or studied the evolution of artificial intelligence and other technologies applications in educational environments.

4. Artificial intelligence, big data and cloud computing oriented applications and advantages in education Sector

AI, big data and cloud computing, all of them are having great abilities and applications of them in different sectors is growing. Here in this paragraph, AI, big data and cloud computing oriented applications in education sector and their advantages are discussed.

4.1 Artificial intelligence-oriented application in education sector

Since the appearance of programming language such as list processing (LISP) which was developed by John McCarthy, there have been so many different programming languages like Prolog, C, C ++, Python, etc. introduced which are helpful in programming different applications.

While on the hardware side there has been incursion of computers with increasingly better resolution and processing capacity. All this has given opportunities to the construction of intelligent applications and systems that can help teachers and students in teaching and learning as well as have personalized learning options for the students.

Grading of exam papers is another area in which AI can extend its help. This help will be phenomenal. AI algorithms are effective. It could review results which could bring out some key observations from the results. This would be good for improvement.

With the development of cloud computing and big data, management and they have made it possible to circulating the flow of information without any restriction, which allowed teachers to intervene remotely in revision activities, reinforcement in the teaching and learning process, thus enhancing the teaching role. AI based smart virtual tutors that support the teaching and learning process are possible.
The presence of virtual tutors who support the teaching and learning process is very comforting for teachers and students. Its application is that it is capable of answering frequently asked questions thus supporting the entire value chain of the teaching and learning process.

Advantages of AI in education sector

- Facilitation of learning with help of different AI built intelligent applications and systems.
- Can make having personalized learning options possible for the students.
- AI can extend help in grading exam papers.
- Results could be reviewed by AI for obtaining key observations.
- AI based smart virtual tutors can help in answering frequently asked questions

4.2 Big data-oriented application in education sector

Through the implementation of big data, the collection of large amounts of data is possible. The accumulated data can then be analyzed after its processing to gain insightful information. In education sector, there is a lot of data generated related to students' studies. The generated data is important.

All the data can be analyzed with the help of big data analytics. This can help in understanding and gaining insightful information and pattern. If consider, data of student's result is analyzed then this can give insightful information on the student's result indicating the progress of the students, how well they are faring in the exam, etc.

Advantages of big data in education sector

- Allows educational institutes the collection of extreme large amount of educational and other related data
- A very large amount of educational and other related data can be stored
- Efficient data management.
- Big data analytics is powerful in analyzing essential data.

4.3 Cloud computing oriented application in education sector

With the development of cloud computing, it is possible to circulate the information and continue the flow of information without any restriction. Any information can be stored at cloud.

It can then be easily accessed by teachers or students or any intended recipient which makes the flow of information easy and possible without any restriction. This is how the flow of information can be carried out without any restriction.

Now for example, consider if the teachers want to share information regarding examination rules, they can then easily put up a circular on the cloud and the students can access and view it from there thus making the flow of information not only possible but very easy.
Likewise various other information can be shared, educational data can be stored and kept secure at cloud, etc. Cloud computing is thus useful in education sector.

Advantages of cloud computing in education sector

- The circulation and flow of information can be carried out effectively without any restriction.
- Any information which is stored at the cloud can be accessed by any intended recipient.
- Any important educational data can be stored at cloud.
- Stored data can be kept secure at cloud.

5. Discussion

AI, big data and cloud computing, all of them are powerful. They all have different applications and advantages in education sector. Through AI, big data and cloud computing, education sector can transform. The advantages education sector will receive from them is a gain for this sector.

However, there could be possibility of some issues and challenges that the continued long-term application of all of them could bring in education sector. There should be preparedness for this.
Solutions need to be found and work is required to be done in order to face and overcome the possible issues and challenges that could occur with continued long-term application of AI, big data and cloud computing in education sector.

Other than this, if this aspect is taken good care of by finding solutions for overcoming the possible issues and challenges then with the advantages from AI, big data and cloud computing education sector will progress well.

6. Conclusion

Application of AI, big data and cloud computing in education sector brings advantages in education sector. They help the education sector in different ways as discussed in the chapter.

Overall, the applications of AI, big data and cloud computing in education seem to be transforming the education sector in a way that benefits this sector. However, there could be possibilities of certain challenges and issues that the long-term application of AI, big data and cloud computing can bring in as discussed above.

One needs to be prepared for this as well and also needs to work on it to face the possible challenges and issues and overcome them with effective solutions. This will ensure AI, big data and cloud computing in education sector benefits it well and helps it develop and grow further.

7. References

[1] Martín, A.C.; Alario-Hoyos, C.; Kloos, C.D. (2019). Smart Education: A Review and Future Research Directions. *Jorunal Proccedings*, 31(57). Doi: 10.3390/proccedings2019031057
[2] Ruiz-Palmero, J., Colomo-Magaña, E., Ríos-Ariza, J. M., Gómez-García, M. (2020). Big Data in Education: Perception of Training Advisors on Its Use in the Educational System. *Social Sciences*. 9(53), doi: 10.3390/socsci9040053. pp. 1-13.
[3] Chassignol, M., Khoroshavin, A. Klimova, A., Bilyatdinova, A. (2018). Artificial Intelligence trends in education; a narrative overview. 7th International Young Scientist Conference on Computational Science. *Procedia Computer Science*. 136, 16-24.
[4] Scalera M. Gentile, E., Plantamura, P. Dimauro, G. (2020). A Systematic Mapping Study in Cloud for Educational Innovation. Applied Sciences. 10(4531), pp. 1-14. doi: 10.3390/app10134531.
[5] Fahad A. Alghamdi (January 2018) An Integrated Cloud model for intelligent E-Learning system. International Journal of Applied Engineering Research. Vol. 13, No. 14, pp 11484-11490.

[6] Neelakantan, P. (2018). A Study on Elearning and Cloud Computing. *International Journal of Scientific Research in Computer Science, Engineering and Information Technology.* 3(1), pp. 1534-1539.
[7] Fischer, C., Pardos, Z. A., Baker, R. S., Williams, J. J., Smyth, P., Yu, R., Slater, S., Baker, R., & Warschauer, M. (2020). Mining Big Data in Education: Affordances and Challenges. *Review of Research in Education,* 44(1), 130-160. doi:10.3102/0091732X20903304
[8] Guan, Chong, Mou, J. Jiang, Z. (2020). Artificial Intelligence innovation in education: A twenty year data driven historical analysis. *International Jorunal of Innovation Studies.* 4 (4), 134-147.
[9] Mali, K., Kothari, N. (2020). Cloud Computing In School Education: A Study Enlightening Benefits and Challenges. *International Journal of New Technology and Research.* 6(5), pp. 17-26.
[10] Palanivel, K. (2020). Emerging Technologies to Smart Education. International Journal of Computer Trends. 68 (2), 5-16.
[11] Raja, R. Nagasubramani, P. (2018). Impact of Modern Technology in education. *Journal of Applied and Advanced Research. 3(*Suppl.1) S33 -S35.

6

Artificial Intelligence, Machine Learning and Deep Learning Approaches as a tool in Breast Cancer Diagnostics

Mridula Moudgil[a], Alka Bali[a] and Nishu Bali[b]

[a]*University Institute of Pharmaceutical Sciences, UGC Center of Advanced Study, Panjab University, Chandigarh, India*
[b]*Department of Computer Sciences, Chitkara University, Rajpura, Punjab, India*

Abstract

Breast cancer is the most fatal and frequently occurring cancer type in females. The diagnosis of breast cancer is done employing diverse imaging techniques like mammography, histological images, magnetic resonance imaging (MRI), etc., which assist the radiologists in detection of abnormalities in the breast tissue. However, these tests have limited capabilities of detection, with possibilities of false negative or false positives. Rapid advancement of Artificial Intelligence (AI) technology has reduced the workload of the histopathologists and radiologists considerably, by increasing the objectivity of the diagnostic tests. Computer-aided diagnosis/detection (CAD) systems are not only reducing the dependency on operators but are also improving the diagnostic capabilities of the sophisticated imaging techniques. Machine learning techniques like Artificial Neural Network (ANN), Convolutional Neural Network (CNN), Support Vector Machine (SVM), Multilayer Perceptron (MLP), etc., are contributing towards enhancing the image recognition capabilities of the modern computer systems, which, in turn, has considerably reduced the number of false positives, thus sparing many women the ordeal of unneeded biopsies/ examinations. Amongst Deep learning methods, the CNN is becoming a standard indispensable image recognition technique, which is also being explored in histopathological diagnosis. The applicability of CNNs to digitized histopathology has been demonstrated for identification of sentinel lymph node metastasis in lymph nodes. Another Genetically Optimized Neural Network (GONN) algorithm has been recently proposed for classifying the database of breast cancer as benign or malignant. This chapter reviews the applications of artificial intelligence, machine learning and deep learning approaches in the field of breast cancer diagnosis and prognosis along with its future implications.

1. Introduction

Breast cancer is recognized as the most common type of cancer in women worldwide and is responsible for largest number of fatalities as well. The GLOBOCAN estimates of worldwide cancer incidence and mortality based on data from 185 countries has shown that female breast cancer outstripped lung cancer in being the most commonly diagnosed type of cancer, with an estimated 2.3 million new cases (11.7%) in the year 2020 and was associated with mortality in 6.9% of cases [1].

A sizeable proportion of women are prone to invasive cancer category with a huge percentage of likely fatalities, which, if detected in early stages, can significantly reduce the mortality rate among the women [2]. Worldwide, varying statistics are reported based on level of development, income, environmental factors, etc. According to a report by the World Cancer Research Fund [3], more than two million new cases of breast cancer were reported in 2018 alone which accounted for about one fourth of the total number of cancers in women.

As per a recent report by IARC (International Agency for Research on Cancer), there were over two million new cases detected in the year 2018. According to the National Cancer Institute, there has been a consistent average annual rise of 0.3% in the new age-adjusted female breast cancer cases from 2008 to 2017. According to the World Health Organization (WHO) factsheet, 2.3 million women were diagnosed with breast cancer in the year 2020, and 685000 deaths were reported globally. However, the age-adjusted fatality rates have been decreasing at a faster average rate each year (during 2009–2018) with a corresponding consistent rise in the five-year relative survival per cent from 1980s to 2012.

According to the current trends, the cases of breast cancer will be rising further and an increase in early detection of the cases will lead to early provision and management of medical treatment for the disease. The modern treatment facilities and advancements made in diagnosing technology have led to a decline in mortality rates of the patients and screening is recommended annually for females above 40 years of age.

Nowadays, breast cancer can be detected as early as 4-6 years prior, using Artificial intelligence (AI) based techniques and medical data which can effectively mimic a physician's ability to diagnose and conclude about a patient's symptoms [4]. This early detection translates into considerably improved chances of survival for the breast cancer patients.

Mammography is a specialized medical imaging technology that employs low dose X-ray system to view and detect changes in breast tissue. Generally, while screening a mammography test, the radiologist is interested in locating a Ductal Carcinoma in situ (DCIS). Abnormalities in mammograms examination like microcalcification, masses and architectural distortion are acute signs for the presence of breast cancer [5-7].

MRI of the breast also plays a major role in detection and management of the disease. Additionally, the cancer classification based on the histopathological and clinical methods are facing many challenges as these methods are prone to incomplete and misleading results [8].

However, the enhancements in the data repositories regarding the test images, diverse healthcare offering, diagnosing time have led to the rapid evolution in the AI and data driven techniques [9]. Certainly, this advancement has positively impacted the accuracy in the breast cancer classification, time response and services provided by health care providers [10-12].

Further, the automations in tumour diagnostic system have been proven to be promising tools thereby, detecting tumours even in the cases that are missed by the expert physicians. AI technology has been embraced in the medical field with enthusiasm due to the positivistic attitude of the clinicians with regard to the inclusion of this technology in the decision-making process [13-15] and hence, it has specifically forayed into the area of Breast Cancer diagnostics (Fig. 1).

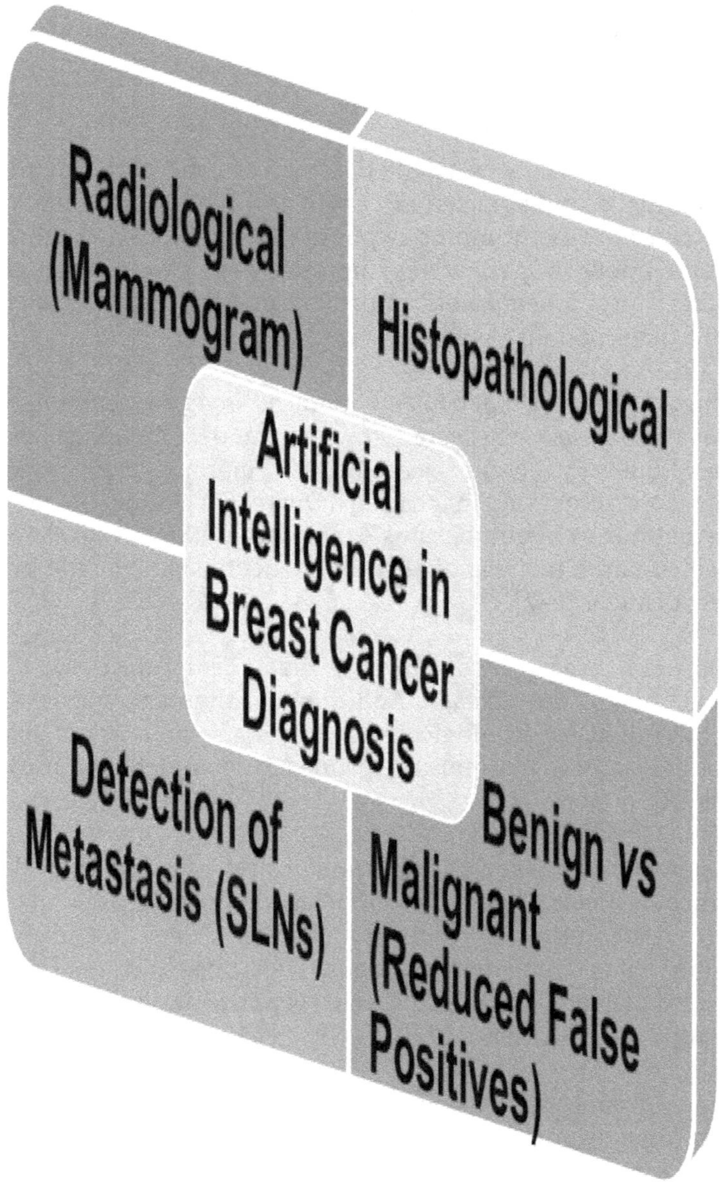

Fig. 1. Artificial intelligence in breast cancer diagnostics.

Machine learning is a subset of artificial intelligence that assists in computer aided diagnosis which comprises of several learning algorithms like SVM (support vector machine), K-means, decision tree, KNN etc. [16]. These algorithms have the ability to learn without being explicitly programmed, in other words, they can serve as a standalone program to estimate the results.

'Neural networks' is a deep learning technique which imitate the working of our brain, where a complex network of interconnected neurons is modelled and in the context of cancer diagnosis, it is made to learn different characteristics of how the cancer looks like [17]. Tons and thousands of mammograms datasets with and without cancer characteristics are introduced to the models as input.

Afterwards, the model is tested using some testing datasets and re-trained again to reduce the error in the prediction and detection. By following this course for a certain iteration, with multiple testing datasets, the model learns the breast cancer trends automatically without human intervention or assistance and can adjust its actions accordingly [18-23].

1.1 Mammography

Mammography is a technique that generates a single 2D-image of the breast (mammogram). Since the turn of this century, digital mammography has been extensively developed and put to clinical use. In this technique, a digital X-ray detector was used instead of an X-ray film resulting in ready generation of a digital image, for evaluation and interpretation by radiologists.

This has not only resulted in a considerably simplified workflow, but the technology has found additional applications towards advanced image acquisition techniques like breast CT and digital breast tomosynthesis.

A mammogram allows the detection of breast cancer even before the actual lump can be felt by a patient. This is described as of two types, screening mammogram and diagnostic mammogram.

The former one is used to look for signs of breast cancer even if the symptoms are not occurring whereas, the latter is used to look for cancer if the woman is showing symptoms or if any change is seen in screening mammogram.

Screening examinations, if performed on asymptomatic individuals, can lead to early detection of the unsuspected disease [24]. As mammography (X-ray-film based as well as digital) acquires two-dimensional images of the breasts, these suffer from lack of accuracy as the malignant lesion may remain masked or hidden by normal tissues.

Moreover, the fibroglandular tissues present in almost 50% of the cases (termed as dense breasts) has been found to evade detection in almost 30-35% of cases [25]. To overcome these problems, two views of both the breasts are acquired and evaluated by a radiologist, i.e., a cranio-caudal (CC) view along with the medio-lateral oblique (MLO) view.

Matching and analysing the two views together can help determine whether a lesion presented in one view is also present in the second view and is not just an artefact or a random tissue presenting suspiciously.

Mammograms are considered as the most dependable method for the detection of any type of abnormalities in the breast tissue, including malignant neoplastic disease.

A radiologist while examining the mammogram images will try to find any sort of unusual changes in the breast tissue, usually done by juxtaposing the recent and the older mammogram and will anticipate for calcifications, masses or other abnormalities that are suspicious or signal the potential of breast cancer.

1.2 Calcification

Calcifications are tiny calcium deposits that are found in the breast tissue. These deposits are found in most of the women, and in a few cases, these could get associated with the abnormalities like cancer. Calcifications are easily recognizable on mammogram images because calcium is excellent at absorbing x-rays from a mammogram [26-27].

There are two types of calcification, first, macrocalcifications, that appear as larger spots on a mammogram, are often age-related, non-cancerous changes in the body and become more common with age. Second are microcalcifications, the most important descriptor to show malignancy while screening. Unlike macrocalcifications, the microcalcifications show up as small spots on a mammogram and are more likely to be a marker for cancer. If microcalcifications are present as clustered distributions, these generally represent malignant cancer, whereas individual MCs usually represent benign cancers [28].

During imaging, the shape, appearance and distribution of these calcifications are investigated in order to ascertain that the deposits are normal calcifications, and not worry-some calcification [29].

Approximately most of the conducted biopsies come out to be normal. However, these deposits can also occur due to hormonal changes in the body (usually after menopause) as calcification is body's own way of responding to the changes.

An area of breast tissue with a distinct shape is usually termed as a mass or a breast lump. Breast masses often have irregular edges, making them easy to spot among the rest of the breast tissue. The two main types of unusual masses are related to cysts or fibrosis.

Former are just the fluid filled sacs whereas, the latter refers to firmness in connective tissue. The cysts are not generally cancerous, however, fibroadenomas (fibrous solid masses) can be more threatening and may necessitate further investigation.
Solid masses usually signify tumors that can be benign as well as cancerous. Fibro-adenomas that are cancerous look no different from the non-cancerous ones and hence, a biopsy is usually necessary to determine whether it's cancerous or not. Some breasts tend to have higher proportion of fibrous or glandular tissue, thus, making them denser.

All breasts are made up of glandular and fibrous tissues, ducts as well as fat. A high breast density is often the result of having more glandular or fibrous tissue in the breast than fat [30]. Presence of dense breasts sometimes makes it difficult to spot masses which can put an individual at a higher risk of breast cancer, especially, at the time of false negatives and the absence of self-examination tests of breasts [31].

2. AI in breast cancer diagnosis: Machine learning

Machine learning is a ramification of artificial intelligence comprising of a broad range of algorithms where models are built up based on a training set taken from an existing database. This algorithm is then used to construct a mathematical model to optimally fit in or to explain the data. Broadly, there are two types of machine learning techniques, i.e., supervised learning and unsupervised learning.

ML basically involves extraction of information (features) or patterns from the provided data for training the model. Subsequent analysis of these patterns or features can classify the abnormalities, followed by applying a suitable algorithm to develop the most suited model to explain the observed data features. Supervised learning approaches like ANN, SVM, KNN, decision tree, random forest, etc. proceed through prior labelling of the data.

In the context of breast cancer diagnosis, this labelling is based either upon pathological or genomic data to identify and segregate different types of breast tumors. The ML algorithm is thus, trained by exposing to these labelled data. The performance of the developed algorithm goes on improving as the training database goes on expanding and thus, availability of well-labelled tumor images is essential to train the model.

In unsupervised ML, the data needs to be classified first, based on similarity of image characteristics. Hence, the database needs to be more sound and larger in comparison to the dataset needed for supervised learning methods.

2.1 Machine learning in tumor classification

Classification of tumors into benign and malignant classes is the most important part of cancer diagnosis, as it determines the further course of action, i.e., biopsy or further screening workup. Due to significant amount of convergence in the appearance of benign and malignant abnormalities, the technique of mammography displays a positive predictive value (PPV) below 35%.

Here, PPV describes per cent lesions submitted for biopsy, which were actually found to be cancerous. In other words, a large percentage of women have to undergo the discomforting and expensive biopsies for otherwise benign lesions.

Various machine learning (ML) techniques and methods are being employed for computer-aided detection (CADe) of potential tumor mass in mammograms with the aim of reducing false positives. CADe was primarily implemented as a second referral, for use during screening to reduce the chances of lesions remaining overlooked by the radiologists.

Further, ML methods have been explored for computer-aided diagnosis (CADx) to distinguish the benign tumors from malignant ones by feeding a 'mass' as an input. The conventional CADe/CADx systems are able to identify and score the suspicion associated with lesions based on certain user-programmed features.

Thus, the grading of lesions by conventional CAD algorithms as suspicious is actually the based on the identification of specific features that have been pre-designated by clinicians as suspicious motifs. Improvements incorporated in CADe algorithms are also practically based on the approaches that a radiologist would utilize to aid him in his diagnosis, e.g., information review of different views taken for the same breast, or by taking matching views of the two breasts.

For example, significant performance improvement in algorithms was noted when provision was made to detect bilateral mammographic density asymmetries across the matching views of the two breasts [32-33]. However, these algorithms could also not hold promise after showing initial successes with limited types of datasets [34].

Moreover, application of CADe was actually found to reduce the positive predictive value (PPV) with concomitant lowered specificity and no improvement in in sensitivity. Data setting measures for increasing sensitivity were further associated with an increased rate of false positives in malignancy identification. Computational tools are made to assist the radiologist and reduce the inaccuracies experienced while examining a mammogram.

ANN (Artificial Neural Networks) is the most widely used tool in interpreting the mammogram and detecting cancer in a biopsy. ANN detects the area by two major methods, first, by improvising directly on ROI (the Region of Interest) and understanding the situation from the features extracted from the pre-processed image signals.

Many computer aided detections using ANN and CNN (Convolutional Neural Networks) are used for diagnosing micro-calcification in the breast tissue. Wang *et al.* [35] have reported a potential clinically viable approach for breast cancer grading based on detection of mitosis by coalescing the supervised feature generation of a data-trained CNN model with handcrafted features capturing various attributes of mitoses, such as morphology, texture, color, etc.

This computationally light approach offers advantages over laborious manual mitotic counting performed by pathologists, and also over the existing automated computerized systems for detection of mitotic nuclei, as the latter are complicated by high variability encountered in the pattern, appearance and presentation of mitoses. Chan *et al.* [36] have reviewed the applications of CAD (computer-aided diagnosis) utilizing deep learning models in breast imaging. Mohebian *et al.* [37] have reported a method for predicting the occurrence of breast cancer in women by analysing the discriminative from the clinical pathological characteristics of a dataset consisting of breast cancer patients having significant prevalence of recurrence.

Further refinement has been carried out by PSO (Particle Swarm Optimization) with ensemble learning (Bagged Decision Tree: BDT). The performance assessment of this hybrid predictor of recurrence of breast cancer has been conducted with holdout and 4-fold cross-validation and comparison with other classifiers like support vector machines has revealed that this model performs superiorly over other tested classifiers.

Usually, these classifications are implemented by pre- processing the image, segmenting it and then applying multi-layer perceptron models with multiple hidden layers and working mechanisms. [38] have proposed deep CNN network architecture named as 'Inception' and GoogleNet (a deep layer network comprising 22 layers) which are credited with the potential of judicious usage of computational resources within the network. This has been done by retaining the same computational requirements whilst increasing the depth as well as the width of the network with results comparable to more complicated models.

This work underlines the fact that improvement in object detection and classification capabilities are achievable with reasonably sized datasets, utilizing lesser number of parameters and average computational facilities by implementation of novel algorithms resulting in improvised network architectures. In other words, results are not just dependent upon availability of powerful computer hardware or inclusion of larger datasets.

Rangayyan *et al.* [39] have reviewed the applications of image processing/pattern analysis techniques for detection of subtle signs of breast cancer.

Agarap [40] has reported a comparison of six machine learning algorithms, i.e., Linear Regression, Softmax Regression, GRU-SVM, Multilayer Perceptron (MLP), Support Vector Machine (SVM) and the Nearest Neighbor (NN) search on a dataset comprising digitized images of Fine Needle Aspirate (FNA) on breast mass taken from the Wisconsin Diagnostic Breast Cancer (WDBC). Training set comprised of 70% of the dataset whereas, 30% was reserved for testing phase. All ML algorithms were found to display accuracy levels above 90%, and maximum test accuracy was demonstrated by the MLP algorithm. The enormous quantities of data present in the databases are difficult to be accessed if done in the conventional way. Data mining is a process of exploring and analyzing large sets of data in order to find a new, hidden or unexpected patterns and rules from the data to predict the future thus providing accurate source for prediction of breast cancer. Large sets of data can either be data warehouses, information repositories or dynamic streamed data [41].

Machine learning, as the name suggests, refers to how well, learning by past experiences (training datasets) can improve the present day decision taking skills (test dataset). The result depends upon the data type and efficiency of the algorithm used.

Decision Tree is another widely used classification tool efficiently following the rules of the tree. It is a supervised machine learning technique consisting of different decision nodes [42], thereby, separating the outcome just like the leaves of the tree according to the parameters defined on the nodes. ID3, CART, C4.5, and advanced J48 are the few classifiers on which Decision Tree can be implemented for good amount of accurate results. Random forest is another advanced extension of decision tree which has also found applications in breast cancer diagnostics.

Bayesian classifiers are the statistical probabilistic classifiers with good accuracy and speed, predicting probability of the particular class. Naive Bayesian (NB) is a type of machine learning classifier algorithm which makes sure that effect of an attribute value is independent from the values for other attributes. It is the simplest and an effective classifier of the text. In the context of breast cancer diagnosis, this can classify an abnormality as malignant and benign with the help of other machine learning techniques. Gaussian Naive Bayes deals with the continuous distribution of data [43-46].

A comparative study was performed using Gaussian Naive Bayes algorithm for classifying the cancer. The algorithm was applied on 2 datasets, first being the dataset taken from the Wisconsin Breast Cancer database and the second being the lung cancer dataset. It had a simple classifier used, which applied the Bayes' theorem, where each attribute was considered as an individual variable. The datasets were trained on the Visual Basic.Net.2013 model for implementing the algorithm. To analyze the effectiveness of this algorithm, the dataset used consisted of breast cancer with 699 instances, out of which, 458 instances were benign and 241 were malignant. Similarly, the lung cancer dataset taken consisted of 1000 instances, of which, 303 cases were of level designated as low, 332 as medium and 365 as high. Further, these datasets were divided into 70% and 30% (training set and test set). Data was classified based on the accuracy, sensitivity and specificity. The results found 98% accuracy in predicting breast cancer. Accuracy of prediction for lung cancer was, however, found to be 90%, as well as, of low specificity and sensitivity, as compared to breast cancer. Thus, Gaussian NB algorithm proved to be more efficient in detecting breast cancer as compared to lung cancer [47].

Support Vector Machine (SVM) is a wide scope pattern classification technique whose accuracy depends upon the input features, parameters accessed and the model structures. It can help in prediction of the disease by examining the genetic profile or the annual mammogram. It works by looking at the extremes of the datasets and draws a boundary between them (e.g., malignant/ benign tumors) [48].

The basic concept revolves around the separating- and the maximum-margin hyperplanes, the soft margin and the kernel function. It acts as a frontier for best segregation of classes [49-50]. Multi-layer perceptron (MLP), a form of ANN, is a field of neural network in which single perceptron is a neuron to the entire network. Multi-layer perceptron neural network is made up of a training dataset comprising of the input data yielding the input layer, one or more hidden layers made of computation nodes, and the output layer comprising of nodes [51]. They require activation functions which help the perceptron to train even the complex neural networks. It also falls under the supervised learning technique and also removes the irrelevant attributes itself.

In another comparative study between various algorithms, the algorithms of SVM, Logistic Regression, Neural Network, Gaussian Naïve Bayes and Voting Classifier were applied to an original Wisconsin breast cancer data set collected by UCI machine learning repository. Voting classifier was reported to be superior as compared to other algorithms, with the highest accuracy of 98.9% [52].

Shah *et al.* [53] have also conducted similar studies on WEKA (The Waikato Environment for Knowledge Analysis) using three algorithms, i.e., Decision tree, Bayesian Network and K-Nearest Neighbor, amongst which, the Bayesian Network was found to be the most proficient, having the highest accuracy (95.9%) and the lowest time consumption. The study utilized a dataset with 699 instances having nine attributes and one class attribute for evaluation.

Woods *et al.* [54] described the idea of segmentation in an image which helped to detect the presence of microcalcifications in ROI. A set of 24 mammograms was analysed at 70 micron resolution with a DuPont NDT scan II Model 35, following which, the segmentation was done and a self-organising ANN called Cascade Correlation (CC) was used as a classifier. The rate of detection of True positives (TP) with CC-ANN for specific micro-calcifications was 73% and for non-micro calcification, it was found to be 92%. KNN (K Nearest Neighbors) is the simplest form of supervised machine learning algorithm which is non-parametric, thus, implying that no assumptions are made. Therefore, it is known as Lazy learner as it simply stores the training tuples and waits for the last test tuple to arrive. It makes its generalizations and performs the classification only subsequent to the arrival of the last test tuple. These stores of training tuples or "instances," are the reason why lazy learners are referred to as instance-based learners [55].

Nearest-neighbor classifiers use distance-based comparisons that intrinsically assign equal weight to each attribute, due to which, they suffer from poor accuracy when irrelevant attributes are given [56-57].

The TP detection rate with CC-ANN was compared with the detection rate of True positive for individual micro calcifications with the KNN algorithm with variable values of K and k. The best results were obtained for K=5 and k=3 having a TP detection rate of 80% for micro calcifications and 84% for non-microcalcifications.

Anitha *et al.* [58] described a morphological mass detection and differentiated the TP (True positive) and FP (False negative) regions by the Wavelet features extracted from the detected mass regions and then comparing them with the features extracted using Gray Level Co-occurrence Matrix (GLCM) with the help of SVM classifier. For SVM classification, the Radial Basis Function is used as a kernel function with sigma value 1. SVM based classifier successfully separated the mass regions from the non-mass regions. The images incorporated in this study were retrieved from the mini-Mammographic Image Analysis Society (MIAS) database. These classification techniques were applied on 45 mass mammograms, amongst which, 43 regions were correctly classified using the wavelet-based detection, whereas 39 regions were correctly identified using the in GLCM based detection. The study concluded that wavelet features with SVM provide improved accuracy rate of 95% in comparison to the GLCM features.

A similar set of studies was conducted by Htay *et al.* [59], in which, KNN classifier was used on the database of MIAS (Mammographic Image Analysis Society). Being a user-friendly interface, MATLAB programme was implemented on the system. The efficient feature extracting was done with the help of GLCM. The results came out to be 92% accurate.

2.2 Deep learning in breast imaging

In recent times, Deep learning has emerged as a significant state-of-art breakthrough technology, with its enhanced capability for object identification and classification tasks leading to high accuracy and robustness. The conventional machine learning methods require a challenging feature extraction stage which is omitted in deep learning methods which can adaptively learn from the provided data in relation to the target output.

These methods are based on several extraction and classification algorithms of AI including the neural networks, amongst which, the convolutional neural network (CNN) is becoming a standard image recognition technique which is becoming indispensable in a number of tasks. The algorithms detection of breast cancer in mammograms rely on the search for soft tissue lesions as well as microcalcifications. Both of these have entirely different characteristics and parameters and not many training datasets are also not available. Hence, the generally used approach is to use separate detection algorithms for these two types of characteristic features followed by combination at last stage of analysis. This approach is exemplified by the two-stage algorithm developed by Lotter *et al.* [60] employing two varying multi-scale convoluted neural networks for masses and calcifications respectively, the results of which are combined to obtain the joint estimate of classification.

CNN was introduced for detection of microcalcifications in mammograms in early nineties [61] and subsequently for classification of mass and normal breast tissue (mass detection) [62]. These models met with encouraging success but needed improvisation for efficient clinical diagnosis of breast cancers. Krizhevsky *et al.* made a mjor foray in this field in 2012, when he won the ImageNet Large Scale Visual Recognition Challenge for developing 'AlexNet', based on 'ImageNet' dataset comprising of more than twelve lakh photographic images which were utilized for training, which was a DCNN (Deep learning convolutional neural networks) consisting of five convolution layers [63].

Excellent competitive performance was demonstrated with DCNN for image classification. In recent times, DCNN is being increasingly applied for a variety of applications in breast imaging, including detection of mass detection, cancer diagnosis and classification, estimation of breast density, identifying microcalcifications, etc. These studies have utilized varying image datasets such as mammograms, ultrasound images, and in a few cases, magnetic resonance images.

Ahn *et al.* [64] designed a CNN based automated mammographic breast density estimator, in which, a total of 397 full field digital mammograms were selected as dataset. Amongst these, 297 were used as training sets and the remaining 100 mammograms were used for testing. The study involved the intensity histogram range within the segmented breast area, which was stretched following an image set generation and patching production.

The training of the CNN model was carried out taking the following:

(i) The local statistic feature
(ii) Histogram set obtained from patch images for the four pre-processed images coupled with the global statistic feature
(iii) The stretched histogram of the complete mammogram along with patch-wise tissue class probability deduced from the binary tissue masks corresponding to each patch image.

An architecture of eight parameters and sixteen layered CNN was trained. The test mammograms were pre-processed and the local and global statistics were extracted and fed into the trained CNN. Finally, the probability of dense tissue value higher than 0.5 was classified and extracted from the trained CNN and the breast density was calculated.

The correlation coefficient of the proposed study, when compared with that of radiologists, turned out to be 0.96, thus highlighting its significant potential in giving a second opinion to the radiologists while diagnosing the mammograms. Nowadays, easy availability of digitized versions of whole slide images has progressed to development of algorithms for computerized image analysis of various types of pathological images for staging of tumors and for proposing patient treatment regimens.

For example, Cruz-Roa *et al.* [65] have employed a CNN (convolutional neural network) to whole slide images of invasive tumors. Here, the classifier has been trained on a dataset of 400 slide images derived from multiple sites and cross-validated on another dataset. This approach has carried out pixel-by-pixel evaluation in contrast to manual annotations and yielded very good predictive statistics (positive predictive value PPV 71.62%; negative predictive value NPV 96.77% and Dice coefficient 75.86%).

These deep-learning based techniques have a significant advantage over conventional CAD as the latter is associated with a high rate of false positives. A major feature that distinguishes these deep learning-based image classification algorithms from conventional CAD is that the algorithm itself determines the image features indicating the presence of a lesion by virtue of its training and this is not input by the person doing the programming.

Otherwise stated, the algorithm is not actually taught about the various features like shape, pattern, texture, etc. of a breast cancer rather, it itself learns what to look for in a breast cancer. During its initial training process, the model is provided various digitized complete/partial images of breasts with the presence and absence of cancer. These images are pre-labelled to designate their status as cancerous or non-cancerous.

During its training, the deep learning network makes progressive adjustments in its internal parameter values in relation to every input image in order to maximize the prediction accuracy status of the image with the truth. This way, the network is able to pick out the image features that potentially indicate the presence of a malignant lesion.

'Wavelets' is the mathematical linear signal processing technique for extraction of information in a more proficient way from the given input having average value zero and limited to the duration. Wavelet Neural Network provides us the advantage of working on non-linear pattern recognition. It recognizes the abrupt pattern or oscillations and smooth regions present in the images and helps in analysis of the data. Thus, it can aid in improving the characterization of pathological images in mammograms [66, 57].

Particle Swarm Optimization (PSO) is the branch of Swarm Intelligence inspired from the patterns and behavior of the nature (for example: flock of birds, immune system as a swarm of cells) [67-68]. Each particle present, accounts as a solution to the problem and group of particles (Swarm) accounts for the collective measures of the solution from which the best optimized results are obtained. It is a population based randomly determined algorithm, for whose execution, it is quite evident that it depends upon the principle of self-organization and division of labor [69].

Deep neural networks consume a significant amount of time and computational resources as they have to be made from the beginning. Junior and Yen [70] have recently developed psoCNN, a novel algorithm that can conduct automatic searches for optimal deep CNN architectures quickly, based on an optimized PSO by employing a variable length direct encoding strategy along with a velocity operator. Good quality performance has been demonstrated with the use of this model.

Dheeba *et al.* [71] investigated a new classification approach using Neural Network based on Particle Swarm intelligence by working on the ROC (Receiver Operating Characteristic) curve. This study employed the mammogram database comprising of 216 images of fifty-four patients, derived from mammogram screening centers.

The entire mammogram set was positive in having abnormalities. Four mammograms were taken per patient, in the Cranio-caudal (CC) view and in the Mediolateral Oblique (MLO) view. These two projections of the right as well as the left breast, were taken corresponding to each case. The identification of doubtful regions was carried out through the various machine learning algorithms, which was followed by their review by expert radiologists. These mammograms were digitalized to a resolution which produced 24 bits/pixel. Every digitalized mammogram was incorporated into a 5.47 Mpixel image.

Screening mammography was conducted on asymptomatic women for detection of clinically occult cancers. The ROC was found to be a satisfactory measure for the proposed detection system as there would be a trade-off between the true positive and the false positive rates (TPR and FPR, respectively). True positive, True negative, False positive and False Negative are the 4 different plausible result outcomes of a single prediction for a two-class type of case (class "1"corresponding to abnormal or malignant cases and class "0" representing the normal cases).

The area under the curve (ROC) was found to be 0.96853 in case of an actual clinical database. The Particle Swarm neural network approach generated good sensitivity and specificity (94.167% and 92.105%, respectively). Rate of misclassification was found to be 0.063291, which was much lower compared to the case when classification was conducted by alternate classifiers. It was also deduced that number of hidden layers inside a wavelet neural network needs to be of optimum count as accuracy varies even if excess (or less) of hidden layers are used to perform the study. In the study, beyond 140 hidden layers, the accuracy was found to reduce by 0.4% using MATLAB version 7.10.

Fuzzy logic is a computational based approach which represents the uncertainties in the continuous set of values. The range of values obtained is entirely different from the binary logic concept [72-73]. In normal terms, it provides the degree of truth between the two answers. It is based upon membership or degrees of membership and is superset of Boolean Principle. It also provides us an advantage of linguistic approach to identify the uncertainty [74-76].

ClaDia a fuzzy rule representing classifier developed by Walter and Mohan 2000 for breast cancer diagnosis. It was applied on the dataset of WBCD. The parameters like nitching, crowding, sterile cache and decision mutations were implemented and thus, best results were obtained compared to other systems. The study yielded an accuracy of roughly 92% and aims for increased fine-tuning performance in the coming future.

ANN trained with Back Propagation algorithm was studied by Saritas [77] using features like BI-RADS (Breast Imaging Reporting and Data System) values, age of the patient and three more BI-RADS features for predicting whether the mammographic mass tissue is benign or malignant. A data of 653 cases were randomly selected as training sets, whereas, 169 were used for testing purpose. Confusion matrix and ROC (Receiver operating characteristic) analysis were carried out in order to assess the success of the study. In the Confusion matrix analysis, out of 344 malignant data, ANN classified 285, whereas, for benign data, 296 out of 349 were classified. These values were found to have sensitivity of 0.843, specificity, 0.834 and an accuracy of 0.838.

On the other hand, when 131 testing cases were presented to the ANN model, 55 out of 68 malign were classified, with 57 out of 63 benign. The sensitivity, specificity and accuracy were 0.902, 0.814 and 0.855 respectively. In ROC analysis, the area under ANN training set was found to be greater than the area under the ANN test data.
When both the results were compared, the sensitivity of the confusional matrix was found to be 90.2% and specificity was found to be 82.4%, whereas the ROC analysis showed the sensitivity to be 80.9% and specificity to be 90.5%, thus, showing that BI-RADS features can be used as input parameters for prediction of breast cancer severity diagnosis.

Several methods are being devised to reduce the complexity involved and time-consumption in the training of deep learning CNNs Transfer learning is one such method, which acts upon the knowledge of the source classifier and extracts information from it to form a new system of classification. Transfer learning is an effective method for circumventing the difficulty of obtaining adequate training datasets for patch- or pixel-level analysis, which otherwise require a time-consuming and tedious process of annotation of images. This classifier has requirement of smaller training datasets along with lesser training time, exactly similar to the way we apply our knowledge of operating one instrument to any other target instrument [78].

This method uses an already-trained deep learning CNN, where a substantial portion of internal CNN parameter values are retained as constant, and only the parameters of the final layers are fine-tuned. In this way, the information from unrelated, very large data sets, like the natural image set ImageNet, consisting of over a million images, can be leveraged in the training of a CNN that is oriented at analyzing mammograms. This permits the usage of information from large unrelated datasets (e.g., ImageNet) to train a CNN for interpreting mammograms.

An effective method of Transfer learning was applied by Chougrad *et al.* [79], using recently proposed CNN models like VGG16, ResNet50 and Inception v3 which were trained with the datasets of Digital database of screening mammography (DDSM), Breast Cancer Digital Repository (BCDR) and Inbreast. These datasets were further combined together to form the Merged Dataset (MD) consisting of 6116 images from 1529 cases using the methodologies of Pre-processing, Applying CNN models, Transfer learning and fine tuning, Regularizing and choosing the hyper-parameters and finally, breast cancer screening framework was formed, thus, categorizing the mass lesions as benign or malignant. Inception v3 came out to be the most accurate (98.94%), followed by ResNet50 (98.77%) and VGG16 (98.64%), when applied on the Merged Dataset. Thus, these were proposed as useful assisting tools in diagnosis.

In a study using data mining techniques [80], three classification models Decision tree, Support Vector Machine (SVM) and Artificial Neural Network (ANN) machine learning algorithms were used to predict the recurrence of breast cancer. Few parameters which were important and left unfilled in the datasets were used by Expectation Maximization algorithm. The latter is an efficient method of extracting estimations from incomplete data.

To predict the recurrence, 24 variables were used in the model. The analyzed data was from the Iranian Centre for Breast Cancer dataset and SVM technique was found to be the best predictor of breast cancer recurrence with maximum accuracy, sensitivity and specificity, followed in order, by ANN and DT. Multi layered perceptron was employed to train the neural networks.

Samala *et al.* [81] have utilized the pre-trained deep learning CNN AlexNet for fine-tuning the network for detection of breast cancer with a very small dataset of around fifteen hundred analog/digital lesion image patches out of which, just 596 were the images containing malignancies. This underlines the power of transfer learning as the original dataset (AlexNet) comprises over 12 lakh natural images. Pruning of CNNs is another simplifying approach which involves decreasing the number of neurons as well as the parameters requiring fine-tuning. This method of pruning should be carried out in such a way that the performance of the final CNN model remains unaffected [82].

A set of 297 digital slides taken from frozen sentinel lymph node sections, segregated into three sets, i.e., training set, development set and validation set by expert pathologists, were used in a challenge competition for development of accurate deep learning algorithms which could have potential applications for per-operative frozen section SLN biopsy [83].

To overcome the issue of limited number of available frozen datasets, Kim *et al.* [84] validated the effectualness of transfer learning from CAMELYON16 for improvising upon the performance of the classification model based on CNN, on a frozen dataset obtained from Asan Medical Center comprising of 297 whole slide images. Effectiveness of three types of models, i.e., ImageNet-based, scratch-based (random initialization), and CAMELYON16-based models was validate through external validation. The best ones were found to be the CAMELYON16-based models (AUC of 0.929 vs 0.919 and 0.897 for ImageNet and scratch-based respectively). The models based on CAMELYON16 displayed higher AUCs for external validation also.
Deep learning CNN has also been combined with hand-crafted features by Kooi et al. [85]. In this comparative study, the performance of CNN was found to significantly improve by incorporating this combined approach, whereas, CNN having access to only image patch demonstrated results no better than the simple conventional CADe method. This shows that aggregation of CNN with conventional CADe can also improve the performance of the model. The combined model is also superior over CADe in the sense that the decrease in sensitivity noted with CADe at low levels of false positives was comparatively lesser on amalgamation with CNN. Ensemble learning algorithm also helped out in predicting the diagnosis. It differs from other learning algorithms, in that it learns more than one type of learning theory from the training data [86-87].

Usual algorithms learn just one theory, whereas Ensemble learning can construct a set of theories from the training data [88]. Ensemble learning algorithm-based Support Vector Model was utilized by Wang *et al.* [89], which was claimed to reduce the variance associated with diagnosis by 57– 69% and increased the diagnosis accuracy by 0.5%-0.9%. The data for analysis was taken from Wisconsin Diagnostic Breast Cancer (WDBC), Wisconsin Breast Cancer (WBC), and the SEER (Surveillance, Epidemiology, and End Results) program of National Cancer Institute (US) for obtaining the breast cancer datasets. Weighted Area under the Receiver Operating Characteristic Curve Ensemble (WAUCE) Support Vector Model used, helped in reducing the variance and increasing the accuracy. The highest accuracy achieved by the proposed WAUCE model for the WBC dataset was 97.10%, for WDBC dataset, it came out to be 96.68%, and for SEER, it was found to be 76.42%. The least accuracy variances obtained was 0.08% for WBC dataset, and 0.22% for WDBC dataset. The results from the study suggested that WAUCE significantly increased the performance for cancer diagnosis.

Nilashi *et al.* [90] used a novel knowledge-based system to classify breast cancer disease by clustering, removal of noise, & classification techniques. The data clustering was carried out by employing the Expectation Maximization (EM) technique and CART (Classification and Regression Trees) was used for generation of the fuzzy rules, used for the classification of the reasoning method based on fuzzy rule. Principal Component Analysis (PCA) was employed to reduce the co-linearity between the data. The dataset was taken from the Wisconsin Diagnostic Breast Cancer dataset and Mammographic mass datasets. After pre-processing of the data, EM clustering was applied to it, and it was further sent for dimensionality and noise reduction to the PCA. CART helped to generate fuzzy rules and these rules helped to make prediction models from each cluster made by EM.

A total of 12 attributes were made in WDBC dataset and the accuracy was found out to be 93.2%. On the other hand, 5 attributes were made in Mammographic mass dataset and accuracy was found out to be 94.1%. These results came out to be the best ones when compared with other machine learning techniques.

Genetically Optimized Neural Network (GONN) algorithm refers to ANN trained using Genetical Programming (GP) parameters. Genetic Algorithm was originally introduced by Josh Holland, prompted by the Evolution Theory by Charles Darwin. This is an evolutionary ML approach involving the classification by selection, crossover, mutations and other attributes. It majorly focuses on the optimization and the robust results [91-92]. By applying the Feed forward neural network yielded by GONN architecture, the prediction of benign and malignant breast cancer can be easily carried out.

A comparison of a performance between various machine learning algorithms such as SVM, Decision Tree (C4.5), NB and k-NN has been carried out by Asri *et al.* [93] based on the original Wisconsin Breast Cancer dataset (WBCD) with an aim to appraise how correctly, data can be classified in terms of effectiveness and efficiency of each algorithm with respect to parameters like precision, accuracy, specificity and sensitivity.

Maximum accuracy (97.13%) and lowest error rate was exhibited by SVM. All experiments are executed within a simulation environment and conducted in WEKA data mining tool. In another study, a comparison of various supervised learning classifiers such as NB, SVM-RBF kernel, Decision trees (J48), simple CART and RBF neural networks revealed similar results as SVM-RBF kernel scored the highest accuracy of 96.84% in WBCD (original) databases [94].

In another comparative study with various data mining algorithms like Sequential minimal optimization (SMO), SVM, BF Tree and IBK, the maximum performance accuracy on the WBC (original) datasets was displayed by SMO. Table 1 below shows Machine learning and deep learning techniques in breast cancer diagnosis.

Table 1. Machine learning and deep learning techniques in breast cancer diagnosis

Reference	Technique Used	Views taken	Accuracy	Dataset used	Advantages	Implemented on
[93]	C4.5	-	95.13%	WBCD	Quick forecast	WEKA machine learning environment.
	SVM	-	97.13%		Accurate	
	NB	-	95.99%		Accurate	
	k-NN	-	95.27%		Fast build up time	
[95]	SSL-dCNN	CC and MLO	82.43%	In-house full-field digital mammography (FFDM) image database	Accurate measure even of unlabelled data.	Modified Le-Net
[96]	SVM	DM	97.71%	The University of Wisconsin hospital Dataset	High performance computing technique	MATLAB version 7.0
[91]	GONN	-	99.63% (60:40 testing: training sets)	WBCD	Remarkable performance	Java and Pentium IV
[97]	SVM	CC and	96.91%	Breast cancer	Good accuracy	WEKA

	ANN	MLO	97.14%	digital repository (BCDR)		
[98]	CNN	CC and MLO	86.1% at 400X magnification	BreaKHis database	Good performance	-
[99]	dANN	-	AUC of 82% (95% CI)	Private	More accuracy	ViDi Suite Version 2.0

Large amount labelled data is an important requirement for training/fine-tuning of CNN. In this regard, methods that could possibly reduce this requirement can lead to simplification. One example is the development of a graph-based semi-supervised learning (SSL) scheme by Wenqing *et al.* [95] (as seen in Table 1) using deep CNN has been utilized for diagnosing breast cancer. Their scheme, comprising of four modules, i.e., weighing of data, selection of relevant features, division of co-training data labelling, and CNN, has the advantage of very small requirement of labelled data for training of the model (in contrast to the usual situation with CNN, where a large amount of labelled data is needed).

Thus, a greater amount of unlabelled data can be used with the proposed scheme in the deep learning algorithm. The scheme utilized 3158 ROIs (regions of interest) containing a mass, prior extracted from 1874 pairs of mammogram images included in the dataset, and except for hundred ROIs, rest were treated as unlabelled. Table 1 shows the medical database for Breast cancer taken from various datasets like WBCD, MIAS, BCDR and other various private databases. After implementing some Machine learning and Deep learning neural network techniques with the help of programs like MATLAB versions, Le-Net and many more, it is evident that these computational tools serve as useful assets for data classification and outcome of breast cancer.

2.3 Machine learning in breast cancer metastasis

A major problem that concerns the clinicians with regard to breast cancer diagnostics is the degree of spread of cancer to other adjoining tissues, i.e., cancer metastasis, and this is an extremely challenging task for the physicians.

Ability to detect the spread of the disease at the earliest stage can be crucial in diagnosis and for exploring the treatment interventions as statistics indicate that above ninety per cent of fatalities associated with breast cancer result from the spread or metastasis of cancer through sentinel lymph node (SLN) circulation to the lymphatic system.

A surgical procedure termed as Sentinel Node Biopsy (SNB) is performed to detect of breast cancer metastases from the original tumor to the lymphatic system. In originating stage, the tumor drains into a few lymph nodes (sentinel nodes) which are detected by injecting tracers for identification of the sentinel nodes containing the migrated tumor cells. Metastasis can be evaluated based on the progression of cancer cells from the elemental region to the lymph nodes and frozen tissue sections of per-operative SLN biopsy are used for confirming metastasis [100-103].

Machine learning techniques have considerably aided the diagnostics by correctly predicting the spread of cancer [104], and generally, Free-Response ROC Curves (AUCs) are used to assess the accuracy of machine learning techniques in diagnosis [105]. Recently, Google has developed LYNA (Lymph Node Assistant) (which is an algorithm based on deep-learning), to accurately identify the regions of metastasized tumors [106].

The study utilized whole-slide images of the lymph nodes of 399 breast cancer patients, stained with hematoxylin-eosin (obtained from Camelyon16 challenge dataset; a public repository) [107]. Amongst these, 270 slides were taken for model development, whereas the remaining slides were taken for evaluation. Very good tumor-level sensitivity (91%) and AUC of 99.6% was obtained with LYNA and results were less affected by histology artefacts resulting from air bubbles, inadequate staining, etc.

However, LYNA needs further improvisation before application to actual clinical situations. This is because, a single lymph node was inspected per patient rather than multiple slides (as seen in clinical cases).

In another study with the LYNA, algorithm assisted pathologists had a significantly increased sensitivity of detection for micrometastases and accuracy was higher when compared to using the algorithm alone or by the unassisted pathologist [108].

Another similar study was conducted by Bejnordi et al. [109] to assess the applicability of deep learning to histopathological whole-slide images (Camelyon16). The study concluded that some deep learning-based algorithms displayed superior performance in diagnostics in comparison to a panel comprising eleven pathologists (with time constraints). Further, the results were comparable to another expert pathologist who interpreted the whole-slide images minus any constraints of time.

3. Conclusion

Breast cancer is a leading cause of death is women and its detection beforehand, can decrease the chances of mortality rates by deciding the medical treatment as early as possible. Current diagnosis relies on mammography for identification of suspicious breast regions, which is then followed by a biopsy of the potentially cancerous breast areas in order to determine whether the suspicious area is malignant or benign).

However, mammography is not entirely perfect at detection of cancerous abnormalities. Hence, radiologists, when unassisted by AI methods, can miss detection of as many as 10–30% of cancers. In recent times, various artificial Intelligence approaches have emerged, that have made the prediction and detection of this disease much more convenient, accurate and trustworthy.

Thus, these form the underlying basis of providing a second opinion to the radiologists or doctors in this context. The areas of Deep learning and Machine learning have emerged as a promising field in the medical sciences.

Classifiers used, if granted access to appreciable amount of datasets for training and testing, can lead to accurate and robust results. If made more feasible and interactive, these will be considered as an asset to the radiologist.

The evolution of better classifiers and statistical algorithms has increased the usage of larger datasets with lesser time consumption and increased accuracy and sensitivity.

In recent years, the predictive performance of various AI-based systems has considerably improved and most of the AI algorithms for detection of lesions and classification, are based on CNNs.

Altogether, AI, Machine Learning and Deep Learning approaches as a tool in breast cancer diagnosis are powerful. Apart from breast cancer, these approaches could also be applied to other medical imaging domains in future.

References

1. Sung, H., Ferlay, J., Siegel, R. L., Laversanne, M., Soerjomataram, I., Jemal, A., and Bray, F. (2021) Global cancer statistics 2020: GLOBOCAN estimates of incidence and mortality worldwide for 36 cancers in 185 countries. CA: A Cancer Journal for Clinicians, 71, 209-249.

2. Breast Cancer Facts and Figures 2019-2020, American Cancer Society, USA, https://www.cancer.org/research/cancer-facts-statistics/breast-cancer-facts-figures.html

3. World Cancer Research Fund (2021) https://www.wcrf.org/dietandcancer/breast-cancer-statistics/ (assessed on 18th May 2021).

4. Shen, L., Margolies, L. R., Rothstein, J. H., Fluder, E., McBride, R., and Sieh, W. (2019) Deep learning to improve breast cancer detection on screening mammography. Scientific Reports, 9(12495).

5. Erbas, B., Provenzano, E., Armes, J., and Gertig, D. (2006) The natural history of ductal carcinoma *in situ* of the breast: a review. Breast Cancer Research and Treatment, 97(2), 135-44.

6. Lehman, C. D., Arao, R. F., Sprague, B. L., Lee, J. M., Buist, D. S., Kerlikowske, K., Henderson, L. M., Onega, T., Tosteson, A. N., Rauscher, G. H., and Miglioretti, D. L. (2017) National Performance Benchmarks for Modern Screening Digital Mammography: Update from the Breast Cancer Surveillance Consortium. Radiology, 283(1), 49-58.

7. Parikh, U., Chhor, C. M., and Mercado, C. L. (2018) Ductal carcinoma in situ: the whole truth. American Journal of Roentgenology, 210(2), 246-255.

8. Morrow, M., Waters, J., and Morris, E. (2011) MRI for breast cancer screening, diagnosis, and treatment. The Lancet, 378, 1804-1811.

9. Arevalo, J., Gonz´alez, A., Ramos-Poll´an, R., Oliveira J. L., and Lopez, M. A. G. (2016) Representation learning for mammography mass lesion

classification with convolutional neural networks. Computer Methods and Programs in Biomedicine, 127, 248-257.

10. Houfani, D., Slatnia, S., Kazar, O., Zerhouni, N., Merizig, A., and Saouli, H. (2020) Machine learning techniques for breast cancer diagnosis: literature review. In: Ezziyyani M (eds). AI2SD 2019. Advances in Intelligent Systems and Computing, 1103, 247-254.

11. Jiang, Y., Edwards, A. V., and Newstead, G. M. (2020) Artificial intelligence applied to breast MRI for improved diagnosis. Radiology, 298(1), 38-46.

12. Slomski, A., (2020). Long-term mortality outcomes in early breast cancer screening trial. JAMA, 324(20).

13. Ramesh, A. N., Kambhampati, C., Monson, J. R. T., and Drew, P. J. (2004) Artificial intelligence in medicine. The Royal College of Surgeons of England, 86, 334–338.

14. Houssamia, N., Kirkpatrick-Jones, G., Noguchi, N., and Lee, C. (2019) Artificial Intelligence (AI) for the early detection of breast cancer: a scoping review to assess AI's potential in breast screening practice, Expert Review of Medical Devices, 16, 351-362.

15. Dembrower, K., Wahlin, E., Liu, Y., Salim, M., Smith, K., Lindholm, P., Eklund, M., and Strand, F. (2020) Effect of artificial intelligence-based triaging of breast cancer screening mammograms on cancer detection and radiologist workload: a retrospective simulation study. The Lancet Digital Health, 2, e468-e474.

16. Hung, P. D., Hanh, T. D., and Diep, V. T. (2019) Breast cancer prediction using spark MLlib and ML packages. ICBRA '18: Proceedings of the 2018 5th International Conference on Bioinformatics Research and Applications, Association for Computing Machinery, New York, NY, USA, pp. 52–59.

17. Erickson, B. J., Korfiatis, P., Kline, T. L., Akkus, Z., Philbrick, K., and Weston, A. D. (2018) Deep learning in radiology: does one size fit all? Journal of the American College of Radiology, 15, 521–526.

18. Lee, J. G., Jun, S., Cho, Y. W., Lee, H., Kim, G. B., Seo, J. B., and Kim, N. (2017) Deep Learning in Medical Imaging: General Overview. Korean journal of radiology,18(4), 570–584.

19. Litjens, G., Sánchez, C. I., Timofeeva, N., Hermsen, M., Nagtegaal, I., Kovacs, I., van de Kaa, C. H., Bult, P., van Ginneken, B., and van der Laak, J. (2016) Deep learning as a tool for increased accuracy and efficiency of histopathological diagnosis. Scientific Reports, 6(6286), 1-11.

20. Aggarwal, R., Diaz, O., Lladó, X., Yap, M.H., and Martí, R. (2019) Automatic mass detection in mammograms using deep convolutional neural networks, Journal of Medical Imaging, 6(3), 031409.

21. Mehdy, M. M., Ng, P. Y., Shair, E. F., Md Saleh, N. I., and Gomes C. (2017) Artificial neural networks in image processing for early detection of breast cancer. Computational and Mathematical Methods in Medicine, 2017.

22. Rodríguez-Ruiz, A., Krupinski, E., Mordang, J. J., Schilling K., Heywang-Köbrunner S. H., Sechopoulos, I., and Mann., R. M. (2019) Detection of breast

cancer with mammography: effect of an artificial intelligence support system, Radiology 290(2), 305-314.
23. Yue, W., Wang, Z., Chen, H., Payne, A., and Liu, X. (2018) Machine learning with applications in breast cancer diagnosis and prognosis. Designs, 2018, 2(2),13.
24. Gøtzsche, P.C., and Jørgensen, K. J. (2011) Screening for breast cancer with mammography. Cochrane Database of Systematic Reviews, 1, CD001877.
25. Birdwell, R. L., Ikeda, D. M., Shaughnessy, K. F. O., and Sickles, E. A. (2001) Mammographic characteristics of 115 missed cancers later detected with screening mammography and the potential utility of computer-aided detection. Radiology, 219(1), 192-202.
26. Morgan, M. P., Cooke, M. M., and McCarthy, G. M. (2005) Microcalcifications associated with breast cancer: an epiphenomenon or biologically significant feature of selected tumors? Journal of Mammary Gland Biology and Neoplasia, 10(2), 181-187.
27. Sickles, E. A. (1986) Breast calcifications: mammmographic evaluation. Radiology. 160, 289–293.
28. Lazarus, E., Mainiero, M., Schepps, B., Koelliker, S. L., and Livingston, L. S. (2006) BI-RADS lexicon for US and mammography: Interobserver variability and positive predictive value. Radiology, 239(2), 385–391.
29. Saad, G., Khadour, A., and Kanafani, Q. (2016) ANN and Adaboost application for automatic detection of microcalcifications in breast cancer. The Egyptian Journal of Radiology and Nuclear Medicine,7, 1803-1814.
30. Boyd, N. F., Guo, H., Martin, L. J., Sun, L., Stone, J., Fishell, E., Jong R. A., Hislop, G., Chiarelli, A., Minkin, S., and Yaffe, M. J. (2007) Mammographic Density and the Risk and Detection of Breast Cancer. The New England Journal of Medicine, 356, 227-236.
31. Pearlman, M., Jeudy, M., and Chelmow, D. (2017) ACOG Practice bulletin clinical management guidelines for obstetrician–gynecologists. Obstetrics and Gynecology, 130(1), e1-e16.
32. Tahmoush, D., and Samet, H. (2007) An improved asymmetry measure to detect breast cancer. Medical imaging 2007: computer-aided diagnosis. Proceedings of SPIE, 6514, 65141Q.
33. Wang, X., Li, L., Xu, W., Liu, W., Lederman, D., and Zheng, B. (2012) Improving performance of computer-aided detection of masses by incorporating bilateral mammographic density asymmetry: an assessment. Academic Radiology, 19(3), 303-310.
34. Lehman, C. D., Wellman, R. D., Buist, D. S. M., Kerlikowske, K., Tosteson, A. N. A., and Miglioretti, D. L. (2015) Diagnostic accuracy of digital screening mammography with and without computer-aided detection. JAMA Internal Medicine, 175(11), 1828-1837.
35. Wang, H., Cruz-Roa, A., Basavanhally, A., Gilmore, H., Shih, N., Feldman, M., Tomaszewski, J., Gonzalez, F., and Madabhushi, A. (2014) Mitosis detection in breast cancer pathology images by combining handcrafted and

convolutional neural network features. Journal of medical imaging, Bellingham, 1(3), 034003.
36. Chang, J., Yu, J., Han, T., Chang, H., and Park, E. (2017) A method for classifying medical images using transfer learning: A pilot study on histopathology of breast cancer. *IEEE 19th International Conference on e-Health Networking, Applications and Services,* pp. 1-4,
37. Mohebian, M. R., Marateb, H. R., Mansourian, M., Mañanas M. A., and Mokarian, F. (2017) A hybrid computer-aided-diagnosis system for prediction of breast cancer recurrence (HPBCR) using optimized ensemble learning. Computational and Structural Biotechnology Journal, 15, 75-85.
38. Szegedy, C., Liu, W., Jia, Y., Sermanet, P., Reed, S., Anguelov, D., Erhan, D., Vanhoucke, V., and Rabinovich, A. (2015) Going deeper with convolutions. IEEE Computer Vision and Pattern Recognition, Boston, pp. 1-9.
39. Rangayyan, R. M., Ayres, F. J., and Leo-Desautels, J. E. (2007) A review of computer-aided diagnosis of breast cancer: toward the detection of subtle signs. Journal of the Franklin Institute, 344, 312–348.
40. Agarap, A. F. M. (2018) On Breast Cancer Detection: An application of machine learning algorithms on the wisconsin diagnostic dataset. 2nd International Conference on Machine Learning and Soft Computing, New York, https://dl.acm.org/doi/10.1145/3184066.3184080 (assessed on 18th May 2021).
41. Chaurasia, V., Pal, S., and Tiwari, B. B. (2018) Prediction of benign and malignant breast cancer using data mining techniques. Journal of Algorithms & Computational Technology, 12(2), 119–126.
42. Navada, A., Ansari, A. N., Patil, S., and Sonkamble, B. A. (2011) Overview of use of decision tree algorithms in machine learning. IEEE and System Graduate Research Colloquium ICSGRC, 2011, 37-42.
43. Banu, B. A., and Thirumalaikolundusubramanian, **P.** (2018) Comparison of Bayes classifiers for breast cancer classification. Asian Pacific Journal of Cancer Prevention, 19(10), 2917-2919.
44. Ting, S. L., Ip, W. H., and Tsang, A. H. C. (2011) Is naïve bayes a good classifier for document classification?.International journal of software engineering and its applications, 5(3), pp. 37-46
45. Gayathri, B., and Sumathi, C. P. (2016) An automated technique using Gaussian Naïve Bayes classifier to classify breast cancer. International Journal of Computer Applications, 148(6), 16-21.
46. Yildirim, P., and Birant, D. (2014) Naive bayes classifier for continuous variables using novel method (NBC4D) and distributions. *2014 IEEE International Symposium on Innovations in Intelligent Systems and Applications (INISTA) Proceedings,* pp. 110-115.
47. Kamel, H., Abdulah, D., and Al-Tuwaijari, J. M. (2019) Cancer classification using gaussian naive bayes algorithm. *International Engineering Conference (IEC), Erbil, Iraq, pp. 165-170.*

48. Wang, H., and Huang, G., (2010) Application of support vector machine in cancer diagnosis. Medical Oncology, 28(S1), 613–618.
49. Huang, C. L,. and Wang, C. J. (2006) A GA-based feature selection and parameters optimization for support vector machines. Expert Systems with Applications, 31, 231-240.
50. Noble, W. S. (2006) What is a support vector machine? Nature Biotechnology, 24, 1565–1567.
51. Ting, F. F. and Sim, K. S. (2017) Self-regulated multilayer perceptron neural network for breast cancer classification. *International Conference on Robotics, Automation and Sciences (ICORAS)*, pp. 1-5.
52. The authors (2019) Application of data mining techniques to predict breast cancer. 16th International Learning and Technology Conference 2019, Procedia Computer Science, 163, pp. 11-18.
53. Shah, C., and Jivani, A. G. (2013) Comparison of data mining classification algorithms for breast cancer prediction. *Fourth International Conference on Computing, Communications and Networking Technologies (ICCCNT)*, pp. 1-4.
54. Woods, K. S., Doss, C. C, Bowyer, K. W., Clarke, L. P., and Clark, R. A. (1993) A neural network approach to microcalcification detection. IEEE Conference on Nuclear Science Symposium and Medical Imaging, 2, 1273-1275.
55. Al-Hadidi, M., Alarabeyyat, A., and Alhanahnah, M. (2016) Breast cancer detection using k-nearest neighbor machine learning algorithm, 9th International Conference on Developments in eSystems Engineering, Liverpool, pp. 35-39.
56. Jabbar, M. A., Deekshatulu, B. L. and Chandra, P. (2013) Classification of Heart Disease Using K- Nearest Neighbor and Genetic Algorithm, Procedia Technology, 10, 85-94.
57. Han, J., Kamber, M., and Pei, J. (2012) Classification: advanced methods, In The morgan kaufmann series in data management systems, Data Mining, 3rd Edition, Morgan Kaufmann pp 327-442.
58. Anitha, J., and Peter, J. D. (2012) A wavelet based morphological mass detection and classification in mammograms. International Conference on Machine Vision and Image Processing, Taipei, pp. 25-28.
59. Htay, T. T. and Maung, S. S. (2018) Early stage breast cancer detection system using GLCM feature extraction and K-Nearest Neighbor (k-NN) on mammography image. 18th International Symposium on Communications and Information Technologies, Bangkok, pp. 171-175.
60. Lotter, W., Sorensen, G., and Cox, D. (2017) A Multi-scale CNN and Curriculum Learning Strategy for Mammogram Classification. *International Workshop on Deep Learning in Medical Image Analysis,* pp. 169-177.
61. Chan, H. P., Lo, S. C. B., Helvie, M. A., Goodsitt, M. M., Cheng, S. N. C., and Adler, D. D. (1993) Recognition of mammographic microcalcifications with artificial neural network. Radiology, 189, 318.
62. Sahiner, B., Chan, H. P., Petrick, N., Wei, D., Helvie, M. A., Adler, D. D., and Goodsitt, M. M. (1996) Classification of mass and normal breast tissue: a

convolution neural network classifier with spatial domain and texture images. IEEE Transactions on Medical Imaging, 15(5), 598–610.
63. Krizhevsky, A., Sutskever, I., and Hinton, G. E. (2012) ImageNet classification with deep convolutional neural networks. Advances in Neural Information Processing Systems, 25, 1097–1105.
64. Ahn, C. K., Heo, C., Jin, H., and Kim, J. H. (2017) A novel deep learning-based approach to high accuracy breast density estimation in digital mammography. Proc. SPIE 10134, Medical Imaging 2017: Computer-Aided Diagnosis, 101342O.
65. Cruz-Roa, A., Gilmore, H., Basavanhally, A., Feldman, M., Ganesan, S., Shih, N. N. C., Tomaszewski, J., González, F. A., and Madabhushi, A. (2017) Accurate and reproducible invasive breast cancer detection in whole-slide images: A deep learning approach for quantifying tumor extent. Scientific Reports, 7, 46450.
66. Paul, R. R., Mukherjee, A., Dutta, P. K., Banerjee, S., Pal, M., Chatterjee, J., Chaudhuri, K., and Mukkerjee, K., (2005) A novel wavelet neural network based pathological stage detection technique for an oral precancerous condition. Journal of Clinical Pathology, 58(9), 932-938.
67. Venter, G., and Jaroslaw, S. S. (2003) Particle swarm optimization. The American Institute of Aeronautics and Astronautics Journal, 41(8), 1583.
68. Zajmi, L., Ahmed, F. Y. H. and Jaharadak, A. A. (2018) Concepts, methods, and performances of particle swarm optimization, backpropagation, and neural networks. Applied Computational Intelligence and Soft Computing, Volume 2018(9547212).
69. Kennedy, J., and Eberhart, R. (1995) Particle swarm optimization. IEEE International Conference on Neural Networks, Australia, pp. 1942-1948.
70. Junior, F. E. F., and Yen, G. G. (2019) Particle swarm optimization of deep neural networks architectures for image classification. Swarm and Evolutionary Computation, 49, 62-74.
71. Dheeba, J., Singh, N. A. and Selvi, S. T. (2014) Computer-aided detection of breast cancer on mammograms: a swarm intelligence optimized wavelet neural network approach. Journal of Biomedical Informatics, 49, 45-52.
72. Zadeh, L. A. (1996) Fuzzy sets. In fuzzy sets, fuzzy logic, and fuzzy systems: selected papers by Lotfi A Zadeh, 394-432.
73. Dutta, P., and Goala, S., (2018) Fuzzy decision making in medical diagnosis using an advanced distance measure on intuitionistic fuzzy sets. The Open Cybernetics & Systemics Journal, 12, 136-149.
74. Abbod, M. F., Keyserlingk, D. G., Linkens, D. A., and Mahfouf, M. (2001) Survey of utilisation of fuzzy technology in medicine and healthcare. Fuzzy Sets and Systems 120, 331–349.
75. Latha, K. C., Madhu, B., Ayesha, S., Ramya, R., Sridhar, R., and Balasubramanian, S. (2013) Visualization of risk in breast cancer using fuzzy logic in matlab environment. International Journal of Computational Intelligence Techniques, 4(1), 114-117.

76. Ali, S. K., and Mutlag, W. K. (2018) Early detection for breast cancer by using fuzzy logic. Journal of Theoretical and Applied Information Technology, 96(18), 5717-5728.
77. Saritas, I. (2012) Prediction of breast cancer using artificial neural networks. Journal of Medical Systems, 36(5), 2901–2907.
78. Chang, J., Yu, J., Han, T., Chang, H., and Park, E. (2017) A Method for Classifying Medical Images Using Transfer Learning: A Pilot Study on Histopathology of Breast Cancer, *2017 IEEE 19th International Conference on e-Health Networking, Applications and Services,* Dalian, pp. 1-4.
79. Chougrad, H., Zouaki, H., and Alheyane, O. (2018) Deep convolutional neural networks for breast cancer screening. Computer Methods and Programs in Biomedicine, 157, 19-30.
80. Ahmad, L. G., Eshlaghy, A.T., Poorebrahimi, A., Ebrahimi, M., and Razavi, A. R. (2013) Using three machine learning techniques for predicting breast cancer recurrence. Journal of Health and Medical Informatics, 4:124.
81. Samala, R. K., Chan, H. P., Hadjiiski, L. M., Helvie, M. A., Cha, K. H., and Richter, C. D. (2017) Multi-task transfer learning deep convolutional neural network: application to computer-aided diagnosis of breast cancer on mammograms. Physics in Medicine and Biology, 62(23), 8894-8908.
82. Samala, R. K., Chan, H. P., Hadjiiski, L. M., Helvie, M. A., Richter, C. D., and Cha, K. H. (2018) Evolutionary pruning of transfer learned deep convolutional neural network for breast cancer diagnosis in digital breast tomosynthesis. Physics in Medicine and Biology, 63(9): 095005.
83. Kim, Y. G., Song, I. H., Lee, H., Kim, S., Yang, D. H., Kim, N., Shin, D., Yoo, Y., Lee, K., Kim, D., Jung, H., Cho, H., Lee, H., Kim, T., Choi, J. H., Seo, C., Han, S. I., Lee, Y. J., Lee, Y. S., Yoo, H. R., Lee, Y., Park, J. H., Oh, S., and Gong, G. (2020) Challenge for diagnostic assessment of deep learning algorithm for metastases classification in sentinel lymph nodes on frozen tissue section digital slides in women with breast cancer. *Cancer Research and Treatment,* 52, 1103-1111.
84. Kim, Y. G., Kim, S., Cho, C. E., Song, I. H., Lee, H. J., Ahn, S., Park, S. Y., Gong, G., and Kim, N. (2020) Effectiveness of transfer learning for enhancing tumor classification with a convolutional neural network on frozen sections. Scientific Reports, 10, 21899.
85. Kooi, T., Litjens, G., Ginneken, B., Gubern-Merida, A., Sanchez, C. I., Mann, R., Heeten, A., Karssemeijer, N. (2017) Large scale deep learning for computer aided detection of mammographic lesions. *Medical Image Analysis,* 35, 303-312.
86. Zhou, Z. H. (2009) Ensemble Learning. In: Li S. Z., Jain, A. (eds) Encyclopedia of Biometrics. Springer, Boston, MA.
87. West, D., Mangiameli, P., Rampal, R., and West, V. (2005) Ensemble strategies for a medical diagnostic decision support system: A breast cancer diagnosis application. European Journal of Operational Research, 162(2), 532-551.

88. Dietterich, T. G. (2002) Ensemble learning. In: *The handbook of brain theory and Neural Networks*, Arbib, M. A., (ed.) 2nd edition, The MIT Press, Cambridge, pp 110-125.
89. Wang, H., Zheng, B., Yoon, S. W., and Ko, H. S. (2018) A support vector machine-based ensemble algorithm for breast cancer diagnosis. European Journal of Operational Research, 267(2), 687–699.
90. Nilashi, M., Ibrahim, O., Ahmadi, H., and Shahmoradi, L. (2017) A Knowledge-Based System for Breast Cancer Classification Using Fuzzy Logic Method, Telematics and Informatics, 34, 133-144.
91. Bhardwaj, A., and Tiwari, A. (2015) Breast cancer diagnosis using genetically optimized neural network model. Expert Systems with Applications, 42, 4611-4620.
92. Aalaei, S., Shahraki, H., Rowhanimanesh, A., and Eslami, S. (2016) Feature selection using genetic algorithm for breast cancer diagnosis: experiment on three different datasets. Iranian Journal of Basic Medical Sciences, 9(5), 476-82.
93. Asri, H., Mousannif, H., Moatassime, H., and Noel, T. (2016) Using machine learning algorithms for breast cancer risk prediction and diagnosis. Procedia Computer Science, 83, 1064–1069.
94. Chaurasia, V., and Pal, S. (2014) Data mining techniques: To predict and resolve breast cancer survivability. International Journal of Computer Science and Mobile Computing, 3(1), 10 – 22.
95. Wenqing, S., Tzu-Liang, T., Jianying, Z., and Qian, W., (2017) Enhancing deep convolutional neural network scheme for breast cancer diagnosis with unlabelled data. Computerized Medical Imaging and Graphics, 57, 4-9.
96. Azar, A. T., and El-Said, S. A. (2013) Performance analysis of support vector machines classifiers in breast cancer mammography recognition. Neural Computing and Applications, 24, 1163–1177.
97. Ramos-Pollán, R., Guevara-López, M. A., Suárez-Ortega, C., Díaz-Herrero, G., Franco-Valiente, J. M., Rubio-Del-Solar, M., González-de-Posada, N., Vaz, M. A., Loureiro, J., and Ramos, I. (2012) Discovering mammography-based machine learning classifiers for breast cancer diagnosis. Journal of Medical Systems, 36(4), 2259-2269.
98. Spanhol, F., Oliveira, L. S. Petitjean, C., and Heutte, L. (2016) Breast cancer histopathological image classification using convolutional neural networks. *2016 International Joint Conference on Neural Networks (IJCNN)*, pp. 2560-2567.
99. Becker, A. S., Marcon, M., Ghafoor, S., Wurnig, M. C., Frauenfelder, T., and Boss, A. (2017) Deep learning in mammography: diagnostic accuracy of a multipurpose image analysis software in the detection of breast cancer. Investigative Radiology, 52(7), 434-440.
100. Sanguinetti, A., Polistena, A., Lucchini, R., Monacelli, M., Triola, R., Avenia, S., Barillaro, I., Di Patrizi, M. S., Boccolini, A., Conti, C., Bistoni, G., and Avenia, N. (2014) Breast cancer micrometastasis and axillary sentinel lymph

nodes frozen section. Our experience and review of literature. International Journal of Surgery, 12, S12-S15.
101. Tvedskov, T. F. (2012) Staging of women with breast cancer after introduction of sentinel node guided axillary dissection. Danish Medical Journal, 59(7), B4475.
102. Choi, S. H., Barsky, S. H., and Chang, H. R. (2003) Clinicopathologic analysis of sentinel lymph node mapping in early breast cancer. The Breast Journal, 9, 153-162.
103. Gipponi, M., Bassetti, C., Canavese, G., Catturich, A., Di Somma, C., Vecchio, C., Nicolò, G., Schenone, F., Tomei, D., and Cafiero, F. (2004) Sentinel lymph node as a new marker for therapeutic planning in breast cancer patients. Journal of Surgical Oncology, 85, 102-111.
104. Golden, J. A. (2017) Deep learning algorithms for detection of lymph node metastases from breast cancer: Helping artificial intelligence be seen. JAMA, 318, 2184-2186.
105. Moskowitz, C. S. (2017) Using free-response receiver operating characteristic curves to assess the accuracy of machine diagnosis of cancer. JAMA, 318, 2250-2251.
106. Liu, Y., Kohlberger, T., Norouzi, M., Dahl, G. E., Smith, J., Mohtashamian, A., Olson, N., Peng, L., Hipp, J., and Stumpe, M. C. (2019). Artificial Intelligence-Based Breast Cancer Nodal Metastasis Detection: Insights Into the Black Box for Pathologists. *Archives of pathology & laboratory medicine, 143 (7)*, 859-868.
107. Litjens, G., Bandi, P., Bejnordi, B. E., Geessink, O., Balkenhol, M., Bult, P., Halilovic, A., Hermsen, M., van de Loo, R., Vogels, R., Manson, Q. F., Stathonikos, N., Baidoshvili, A., van Diest, P., Wauters, C., van Dijk, M., and van der Laak, J. (2018) 1399 H&E-stained sentinel lymph node sections of breast cancer patients: the CAMELYON dataset. GigaScience, *7*(6), 1-8.
108. Steiner, D. F., MacDonald, R., Liu, Y., Truszkowski, P., Hipp, J. D., Gammage, C., Thng, F., Peng, L., and Stumpe, M. C. (2018) Impact of deep learning assistance on the histopathologic review of lymph nodes for metastatic breast cancer. The American Journal of Surgical Pathology, 42(12), 1636-1646.
109. Bejnordi, B. E., Veta, M., Johannes van Diest, P., Karssemeijer, N., and Venancio, R. (2017) Diagnostic assessment of deep learning algorithms for detection of lymph node metastases in women with breast cancer. *The Journal of the American Medical Association,* 318, 2199-2210.

7

Non-Invasive Method of Heart Rate Detection using Smart Phone by Palm Video Imaging

S.N. Kumar[1], A. Lenin Fred[2], L.R. Jonisha Miriam[3], S.R. Santhiya[4], H. Ajay Kumar[5] and Christina Jane I.[6]

[1]*Amal Jyothi College of Engineering, Kanjirapally, Kerala, India*
[2,3,4,5,6]*Mar Ephraem College of Engineering and Technology, Marthandam, Tamil Nadu, India*

Abstract

Heart rate is an important indicator of a human's healthy life. Numerous methods exist to measure heart rate, but invasive methods are sometimes not applicable in all scenarios or in other words, it is sometimes not possible to have the option of using invasive method for heart rate detection. The non-invasive technology can be the solution in such scenarios and can overcome the difficulty. This work contributes to the solutions that work on the non-invasive method of heart rate detection from video captured by a smartphone. In the work presented in this book chapter, video of the palm is taken as input, the green video frames are extracted from the input video for analysis. After series of the process including brightness signal computation, bandpass filtering is applied in the preprocessing phase. The fast Fourier transform along with the sliding window analysis and peak detection was carried out on the bandpass filtered output for the detection of heart rate. The powerful frequency band is extracted to calculate the heart rate; it produces a 1 beat increment in every value because of using a 6s window for sliding window analysis. The heart rate was estimated in real-time by acquiring palm video and for comparative analysis, the manual technique was also used. The medical person was involved in the manual estimation of heart rate. The heart rate was estimated as follows; resting period, followed by exercise. The heart rate was estimated in two cases for male and female persons. The accuracy was also estimated between the manual and machine-generated reading. The proposed non-invasive method is beneficial, since it does not require any special gadget or separate special camera for heart rate detection. Video of the palm captured by any smartphone camera where the palm is visible is sufficient enough to be taken as input. Hence the proposed non-invasive method for heart rate detection is truly very beneficial.

1. Introduction

Heart rate (HR) is an important indicator of a human's healthy life. HR is one of the simplest cardiovascular parameters; it indicates how many times the heart beats per minute (bpm). Currently, an increasing number of humans are suffering from cardiovascular diseases [1]. The Electrocardiography (ECG) machine is specialist hardware that is being used to measure the cardiac pulse. In this, ECG signals could be extracted via capacitive electrodes attached to the body.

It not only detects the motion artifacts but also discards the identified artifacts, by adding additional electrodes [2]. However, ECG-based methods need to apply gel patches or attach electrodes on the patient's body; these are uncomfortable and create some irritation. Photoplethysmography (PPG) is worked based on the concept of intensity variations in blood [3]. The heart rate could be detected from the plethysmographic signals, which are acquired from the recorded video.

Opto-electronic methods are employed to analyze the lightning variations; here the IR light absorbance may change due to the blood pressure [4]. Nevertheless, in a real-time scenario due to the environmental noise, the PPG signal will get affected this can decrease the heart rate accuracy [5].

The thermal signal-based pulse rate detection method is presented in [6]; cardiac pulses are estimated from blood vessels near the skin surface. In [7], the authors use a thermal camera to measure the breath rate and pulse rate via bioheat techniques.

A time-lapse image-based respiratory and heart rate detection by Charged Coupled Device was proposed in [8], it gives flexible ambulatory parameters for the application like the home healthcare system. Pulse rate detecting system from head movement video based on Ballistocardiogram (BCG) was proposed in [9].

BCG based heart rate detection by using a deformable face fitting algorithm was put forward in [10], the heart rate was estimated from head motion videos subjected to principal component analysis [11]. The BCG based approach relies on the cyclic motion of the head. BCG method is failed for dynamic scenarios, because of the inconsistent feature extraction.

The facial video with PPG, allowing ambient light to measure HR was highlighted in [12]; then it can be improved to the next level as an automatic system with the help of a mobile phone camera [13].

The key idea to measure HR was blind source separation (BSS), which is based on temporal variations in the region of interest (ROI) color. In [14], a modified framework for HR measurement was proposed; it works under realistic situations.

The HR detection technique comprises of three stages: Discriminative response map filtering; normalized least mean square (NLMS) adaptive filtering; and finally, the signal is segmented with SD values. A heart rate measuring system using face video of the person called HiBeat was described in [15]. The proposed HiBeat system is cost-effective. BVP signals from the face could be extracted by using Independent Component Analysis (ICA) [13, 16] and Principle Component Analysis (PCA) [11] to detect the HR.

Numerous video-based non-invasive HR detection approaches were proposed in recent research works. Currently, the most widely used heart rate detecting system is done by smartphones from ROI such as face [12, 13], forehead [17], and cheek [8].

In [18], the human face video was captured, and the blind source separation of R, G, and B frames were carried out using independent component analysis for the detection of heart rate, the results were found to be superior even in the presence of artifacts.

The independent component analysis of the facial video for heart rate detection was also proposed in [19] and is suggesting that smartphones can also be used for heart rate detection. In this research work, the palm area is chosen as ROI and that was preprocessed with a high camera sampling rate to measure the HR that overcomes the drawbacks mentioned earlier without artifacts, allowing variation in the illumination of light over time.

The chapter organization is as follows; section 2 highlights the data acquisition and the video processing of palm for heart beta detection, section 3 depicts the results and discussion and finally, conclusion is drawn in section 4.

2. Methods and materials

This section comprises data acquisition and computational algorithms employed for the detection of heart rate from the palm video. The signal, image, or video, when acquired from an acquisition system are subjected to noise, and hence preprocessing is a vital stage required before any subsequent operation.

The acquired videos are preprocessed by a bandpass filter and subjected to fast Fourier transform with sliding window analysis for the detection of heartbeat.

2.1 Data acquisition

In this study, the test videos for heart rate detection are acquired using a mobile phone (Samsung A50) camera. Test videos are recorded at 29 frames per second with resolution of 1920 × 1080 pixels for 10 seconds.
The test videos are acquired in a natural, isolated environment with different lighting sources. The recorded video is saved in .mp4 format. The area of the palm was chosen as the Region of Interest (ROI).

2.2 Computational algorithms for the processing of palm video to detect the heart rate

The flow diagram of the computational model for the detection of heartbeat is depicted in Figure1. After the video acquisition, it is necessary to ensure the brightness variation in all pixels so merge all pixels in the ROI to an average brightness value per frame.

The recorded video contains RGB frames, but green frames are only considered for real time implementation because the most amount of energy is available in it; hemoglobin pigment in the blood strongly absorbed light with 550 nm wavelengths which belong to the green frame [19].

Hence, green color frames of the video images can be used to detect the variations in the heart rates. So, the green brightness function for n number of samples is expressed in (1).

$$b[n] = \frac{1}{I_w . I_h} v[n, x, y, 1] \qquad (1)$$

where I_w is the width of the image in pixels, I_h is the height of the image in pixels, and $v[n, x, y, 1]$ is the light level of the green frame at x and y coordinates of frame n in the video signal.

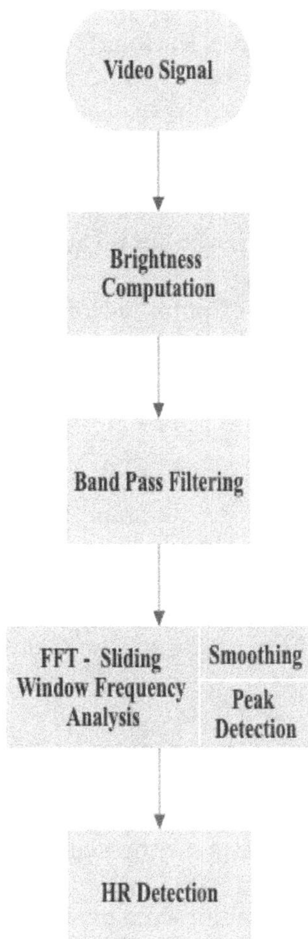

Figure 1. Flow diagram of heart rate detection.

The noise sources are difficult to control especially if someone else operates the system, we can increase the signal level by illuminating the palm area with a stable light source.

It is necessary to measure the signal quality by calculating the signal-to-noise ratio of the region of interest towards the recorded video. For further processing steps, high SNR value is essential to indicate the signal should be strong. After the signal acquisition, a band-pass filter is applied; it attenuates the frequencies outside the required band.

According to the United States National Institute of Health (NIH), the normal human heartbeat is between 60 and 200 bpm, depending on age, fitness condition, and the physical activity that she or he is doing. The periodic signal can be estimated between 40 and 230 bpm, in terms of frequency 0.667 and 3.833 Hz. The whole range of heart rate frequencies could be extracted based on the Nyquist criteria, i.e., the sampling frequency 7.667Hz should be at least twice the highest.

For improving accuracy, the Signal to Noise Ratio (SNR) is the essential factor; that can be increased by maximizing the signal power or minimizing the noise. Noise can be reduced by filtering and make the signal smoother.

A second-order Butterworth filter is chosen because of two reasons, less computation; it provides flat bands. Butterworth filter is required to entirely avoid the signal offset.
Next, the filtered signal utilizes the fast Fourier transform to change the signal to frequency domain. The transformed signal contains both magnitude and phase, here phase is not considered in order to reduce the complexity.

For providing continuous measurement of the heart rate, two processing steps are followed; namely, peak detection and smoothing, these steps are repeated every half seconds. This estimation relies on the 6s window which moves over the signal.

The window length is a major concern because it affects the frequency resolution and accuracy of the HR. The sampling is done through the following sampling frequency,

$$F_r = \frac{F_S}{N} = \frac{\frac{N}{T_W}}{N} = \frac{1}{T_W} \tag{2}$$

where F_s is the sampling frequency, N is the number of window samples, F_r is the frequency resolution, and T_w is window time duration.

The frequency analysis and time evolution of the detected heart rate can be observed after peak detection and signal smoothening.

The highest amplitude is considered as the peak value and corresponds to the pulse rate.

Window duration is one of the important factors to achieve an accurate result. It affects the time accuracy.

Finally, the powerful frequency band is extracted to calculate the HR. It produces a 1 beat increment in every value because of using a 6s window for sliding window analysis.

To get the rapid change in the heart rate 1 bpm resolution frequency is used.

Finally, heart rate can be measured by using (3, 4, 5) from the smoothened peak value.

$$\boldsymbol{C_k} = \sum_{n=0}^{N-1} \boldsymbol{b_n e^{j2\pi n(f_p - 0.5F_r + kF'_r)/F_s}} \tag{3}$$

$$\boldsymbol{U} = \left\{\boldsymbol{0}, \dots, \frac{\boldsymbol{F_r}}{\boldsymbol{F'_r}}\right\}, \boldsymbol{k} \in \boldsymbol{U} \tag{4}$$

$$\boldsymbol{HR} = \boldsymbol{f_p} - \boldsymbol{0.5F_r} + \boldsymbol{F'_r} \operatorname{\mathbf{arg\,max}} |\boldsymbol{c_k}|, \boldsymbol{k} \in \boldsymbol{U} \tag{5}$$

where, *HR* is smoothed heart rate, $\boldsymbol{b_n}$is *k*th sample of brightness signal, $\boldsymbol{f_p}$ is FFT peak frequency, $\boldsymbol{F_r}$ is FFT frequency resolution and $\boldsymbol{F'_r}$ is smoothing frequency resolution, *N* is window length in samples.

The computation complexity was reduced by the factor complexity reduction factor (*CRF*). So, *CRF* is given in equation (6).

$$\left.\begin{array}{r} S = F_r/F_r' \\ F_r' = F_s/N_Z \\ F_r = F_s/N \end{array}\right] \rightarrow S = N_Z/N \rightarrow S.N = N_z$$

$$CRF = \frac{N_Z.\log_2(N_Z)}{S.N} = \frac{N_Z.\log_2(N_Z)}{N_Z} = \log_2(N_z) = \log_2\left(\frac{F_S}{F_r'}\right) \quad (6)$$

where *CRF* is the Complexity Reduction Factor of the partial DFT method over the FFT on the zero padded signal, F_S is the sampling frequency, F_r is frequency resolution before smoothing, F_r' is desired frequency resolution before smoothing, N is window length, N_z is zero-padded window length and S is the number of test tones.

3. Results and Discussion

The proposed method was implemented using MATLAB-2015b. During, development tests were run the following system specification; Processor-AMDA4-4300M APU with Radeon (tm) and 2GB RAM.

Figures 2 and 3 depict the frequency analysis and time evolution of the detected heart rate after smoothing and peak detection from palm video. The testing results of 8 persons are highlighted here.

The readings were calculated before exercise that is in rest condition and after exercise. The running exercise for 5 minutes was done by all the 8 persons, after the rest state and again the readings were noted.

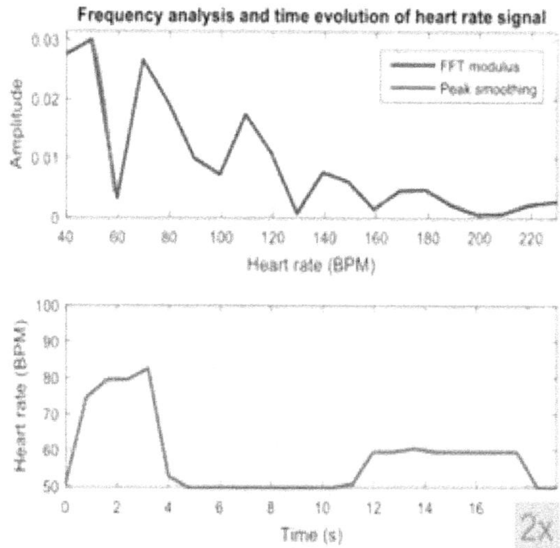

(a) Person 1 at rest

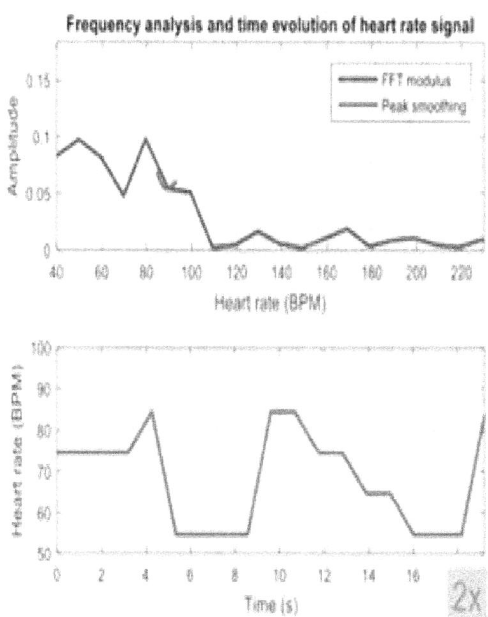

(b) Person 1 after exercise

Figure 2. The frequency analysis and time evolution of the detected heart rate for person 1 at rest and after exercise.

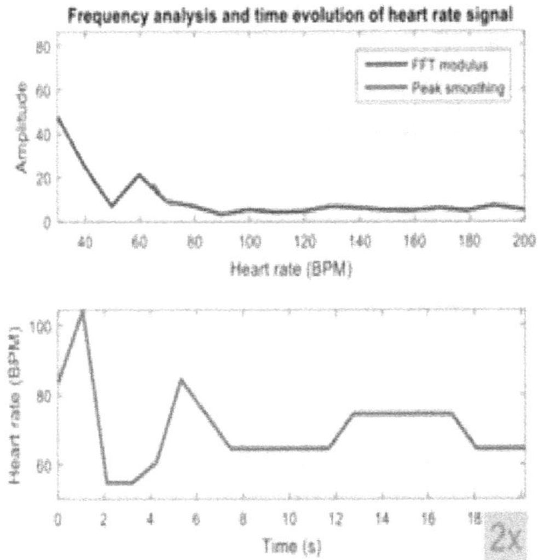

(c) Person 2 at rest

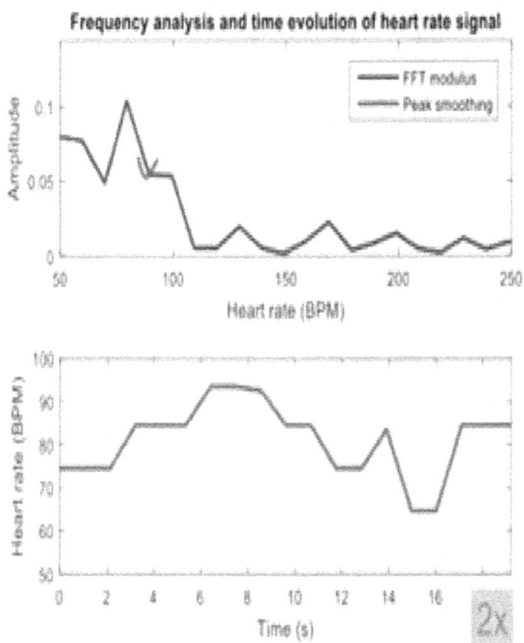

(d) Person 2 after exercise

Figure 3. The frequency analysis and time evolution of the detected heart rate for person 1 and 2 at rest and after exercise.

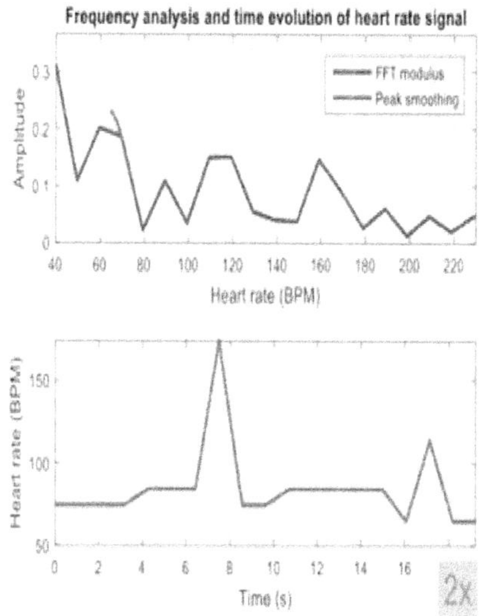

(e) Person 3 at rest

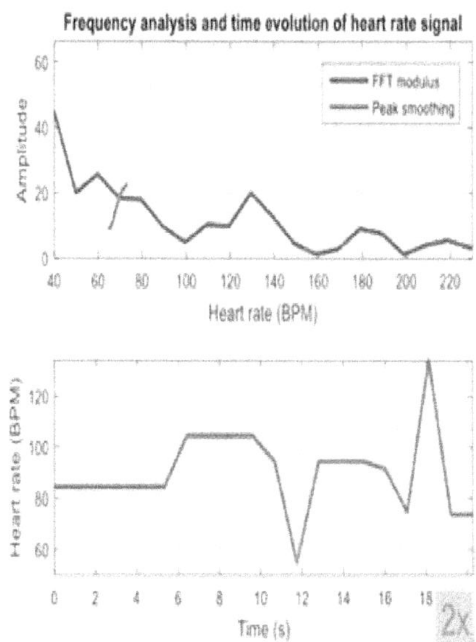

(f) Person 3 after exercise

Figure 4. The frequency analysis and time evolution of the detected heart rate for person 3 at rest and after exercise.

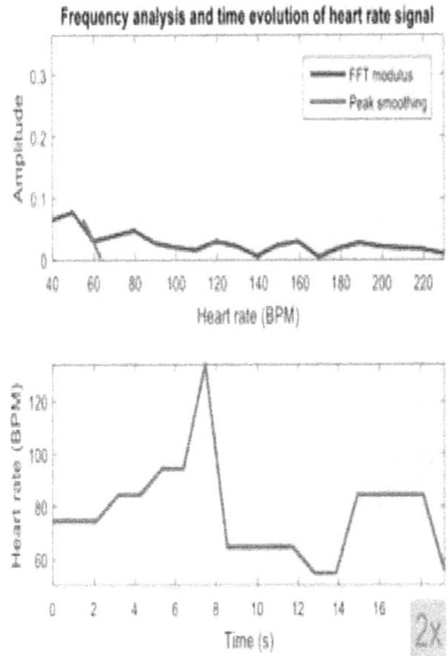

(g) Person 4 at rest

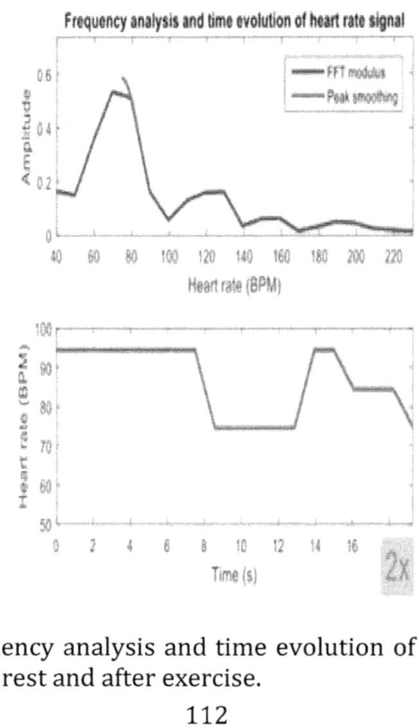

Figure 5. The frequency analysis and time evolution of the detected heart rate for person 4 at rest and after exercise.

Table 1 contains the detected heart rate (by proposed method) and the manual heart rate (by counting heart beats for one minute, manually) for 8 healthy volunteers.

This part of the validation has a focus on the relative accuracy of the values to estimate manually, with the help of Stethoscope while videos were being acquired. The formula for calculating this error is given by the following equation (7).

$$Accuracy = \frac{100*|A-M|}{A} \tag{7}$$

where A is accurate heart rate (manual measurement), M *is* measured heart rate by the proposed method. The proposed method provides acceptable results.

Table 1. Detected heart rate and manual heart rate

	Gender	**Condition**	**Manual Reading (bpm)**	**Experiment Reading (bpm)**
Person 1	Female	At Rest	62	57.7737
		After Exercise	71	68.9806
Person 2	Female	At Rest	72	70.3214
		After Exercise	80	81.0947
Person 3	Male	At Rest	81	84.4857
		After Exercise	89	90.21
Person 4	Male	At Rest	75	77.6827
		After Exercise	85	86.5679
Person 5	Female	At Rest	70	70.2
		After Exercise	75	79.7667
Person 6	Female	At Rest	68	67.669
		After Exercise	78	80.76
	Male	At Rest	82	88.8
		After Exercise	88	92.709

Person 7				
Person 8	Male	At Rest	83	84.586
		After Exercise	89	95.8548

The inferences from the related works for the noninvasive method of heart rate detection are as follows; camera or webcam is required in many cases for capturing the facial video [13] [18], an infrared sensor is utilized in [20] and IoT based wearable systems are deployed in [21]. This chapter proposes a technique that requires a smartphone only for the capturing of palm video and does not require any extra sensors or accessories.

Moreover, the capturing of face video is a crucial thing in the current pandemic scenario especially since everyone has to wear the mask and it's a mandatory thing when people are going outside.

Concerning the feasibility, the proposed research work captures palm video, and the heart rate monitoring can be done anywhere even in public places also with smartphones. It is not always possible to take a special separate camera or a smart gadget for detection of heart rate.

The features of the proposed smartphone-based heart rate detection are as follows:

- Eases measure of heart rate without the use of additional equipment's
- Heart rate can be measured in any public place and can be measured when one is sleeping too.
- The proposed method of heart rate detection is simple and useful as smartphones are a part of life of most of the people in this modern world.

Though there is a variation in the manual reading and the experimental reading estimated by the proposed method, in the future the error can be minimized by an intelligent computational algorithm.

4. Conclusion

In this research work, heart rate is extracted from palm video by video imaging techniques. The proposed method was developed in a non-invasive manner using a smartphone. It provides acceptable results and was compared with manually estimated heart rate values. The proposed research work employs palm video for heart rate detection and gains prominence in the current pandemic scenario, the future work will be focusing on the minimization of error by improving the computational algorithm.

Acknowledgment

The author Dr. S.N Kumar would like to acknowledge the support from the Schmitt Centre of Biomedical Instrumentation of Amal Jyothi College of Engineering.

References

1. Allen, J. (2007) 'Photoplethysmography and its application in clinical physiological measurement', *Physiological Measurement*, 28(3), pp. 1–5. doi: 10.1088/0967-3334/28/3/R01.
2. Balakrishnan, G., Durand, F. and Guttag, J. (2013) 'Detecting pulse from head motions in video', *Proceedings of the IEEE Computer Society Conference on Computer Vision and Pattern Recognition*, pp. 3430–3437. doi: 10.1109/CVPR.2013.440.
3. Boccanfuso, L., Perez, E. J., Robinson, M., & O'Kane, J. M. (2012) 'Collecting heart rate using a high precision, non-contact, single-point infrared temperature sensor', *Lecture Notes in Computer Science (including subseries Lecture Notes in Artificial Intelligence and Lecture Notes in Bioinformatics)*, 7621 LNAI, pp. 86–97. doi: 10.1007/978-3-642-34103-8_9.
4. Garbey, M., Sun, N., Merla, A., & Pavlidis, I. (2007) 'Contact-free measurement of cardiac pulse based on the analysis of thermal imagery', *IEEE Transactions on Biomedical Engineering*, 54(8), pp. 1418–1426. doi: 10.1109/TBME.2007.891930.
5. Khong, W. L., Rao, N. S. V. K. and Mariappan, M. (2017) 'Blood pressure measurements using non-contact video imaging techniques', *Proceedings - 2017 IEEE 2nd International Conference on Automatic Control and Intelligent Systems, I2CACIS 2017*, 2017-Decem, pp. 35–40. doi: 10.1109/I2CACIS.2017.8239029.
6. Lewandowska, M., Rumiński, J., Kocejko, T., & Nowak, J. (2011) 'Measuring pulse rate with a webcam - A non-contact method for evaluating cardiac

activity', *2011 Federated Conference on Computer Science and Information Systems, FedCSIS 2011*, pp. 405–410.
7. Li, X., Chen, J., Zhao, G., & Pietikainen, M. (2014) 'Remote heart rate measurement from face videos under realistic situations', *Proceedings of the IEEE Computer Society Conference on Computer Vision and Pattern Recognition*, pp. 4264–4271. doi: 10.1109/CVPR.2014.543.
8. Pavlidis, I., Dowdall, J., Sun, N., Puri, C., Fei, J., & Garbey, M. (2007) 'Interacting with human physiology', *Computer Vision and Image Understanding*, 108(1–2), pp. 150–170. doi: 10.1016/j.cviu.2006.11.018.
9. Poh, M.-Z., McDuff, D. J. and Picard, R. W. (2010) 'Non-contact, automated cardiac pulse measurements using video imaging and blind source separation', *Optics Express*, 18(10), p. 10762. doi: 10.1364/oe.18.010762.
10. Rahman, H., Ahmed, M. U. and Begum, S. (2016) 'Non-Contact Heart Rate Monitoring Using Lab Color Space.', in *pHealth*, pp. 46–53.
11. Saragih, J. M., Lucey, S. and Cohn, J. F. (2011) 'Deformable model fitting by regularized landmark mean-shift', *International Journal of Computer Vision*, 91(2), pp. 200–215. doi: 10.1007/s11263-010-0380-4.
12. Shan, L. and Yu, M. (2013) 'Video-based heart rate measurement using head motion tracking and ICA', in *2013 6th International Congress on Image and Signal Processing (CISP)*, pp. 160–164.
13. Shin, K. Y., Lee, J. S. and Jang, J. (2016) 'Highly sensitive, wearable and wireless pressure sensor using free-standing ZnO nanoneedle/PVDF hybrid thin film for heart rate monitoring', *Nano Energy*, 22, pp. 95–104. doi: 10.1016/j.nanoen.2016.02.012.
14. Takano, C. and Ohta, Y. (2007) 'Heart rate measurement based on a time-lapse image', *Medical Engineering and Physics*, 29(8), pp. 853–857. doi: 10.1016/j.medengphy.2006.09.006.
15. Temko, A. (2017) 'Accurate Heart Rate Monitoring during Physical Exercises Using PPG', *IEEE Transactions on Biomedical Engineering*, 64(9), pp. 2016–2024. doi: 10.1109/TBME.2017.2676243.
16. Thayer, J. F., Yamamoto, S. S. and Brosschot, J. F. (2010) 'The relationship of autonomic imbalance, heart rate variability and cardiovascular disease risk factors', *International Journal of Cardiology*, 141(2), pp. 122–131. doi: 10.1016/j.ijcard.2009.09.543.
17. Thiagarajan, S. and Balleda, K. (2015) 'HiBeat: A novel highly accurate implementation of cardiac pulse measurement on a multicore architecture', *2014 International Conference on High Performance Computing and Applications, ICHPCA 2014*, pp. 12–15. doi: 10.1109/ICHPCA.2014.7045358.
18. Verkruysse, W., Svaasand, L. O. and Nelson, J. S. (2008) 'Remote plethysmographic imaging using ambient light', *Optics Express*, 16(26), p. 21434. doi: 10.1364/oe.16.021434.
19. Wartzek, T., Eilebrecht, B., Lem, J., Lindner, H. J., Leonhardt, S., & Walter, M. (2011) 'ECG on the road: Robust and unobtrusive estimation of heart rate', *IEEE Transactions on Biomedical Engineering*, 58(11), pp. 3112–3120. doi: 10.1109/TBME.2011.2163715.

20. Yu, Y. P., Kwan, B. H., Lim, C. L., Wong, S. L., & Raveendran, P. (2013) 'Video-based heart rate measurement using short-time Fourier transform', *ISPACS 2013 - 2013 International Symposium on Intelligent Signal Processing and Communication Systems*, pp. 704–707. doi: 10.1109/ISPACS.2013.6704640.
21. Zhang, Z., Pi, Z. and Liu, B. (2015) 'TROIKA: A general framework for heart rate monitoring using wrist-type photoplethysmographic signals during intensive physical exercise', *IEEE Transactions on Biomedical Engineering*, 62(2), pp. 522–531. doi: 10.1109/TBME.2014.2359372.

8

A Voyage on Medical Image Compression Algorithms Based on Mathematical Transforms for Telemedicine Applications

S.N. Kumar, P.C. Thomas, Rahul Robin Baby, T.M. Appumon, Sebin Varghese and Steve Mathew

Amal Jyothi College of Engineering, Kottayam, Kerala, India

Abstract

Image compression plays a dynamic role in minimizing the file size and thereby aids telemedicine for data storage and transfer. The work presented in this book chapter focuses on the mathematical transform-based compression techniques for medical images and in this current COVID 19 scenario, telemedicine is gaining prominence. The Fourier and Wavelet transform are classical mathematical transforms that find applications in preprocessing, segmentation, compression and classification. Variants of mathematical transforms gain prominence in image compression. This work focuses mainly on the role of mathematical transforms for medical image compression. The chapter organization is as follows; need for compression in the medical field, related works, compression algorithms based on mathematical transforms and finally future works. The performance validation of compression algorithms is also discussed in this work. The outcome of this work is helpful in choosing an appropriate algorithm for telemedicine applications.

1. Introduction

Image processing utilizes computer-aided algorithms to analyze images and extract valid information beneficial to the user [1]. Image processing gains prominence in the medical and remote sensing domain. In the medical field, image processing techniques aids physicians and surgeons to process and analyze medical images for disease diagnosis and therapeutic planning. Compression algorithms are utilized to reduce the file size and gain importance in teleradiology for data transfer. The medical images obtained from the acquisition systems like scanners are in Digital Imaging and Communications in Medicine (DICOM) or Raw format [2].

For a single patient itself, a scanning process results in 200 to 500 images and varies that depends on the setting by the radiologist. The storage and transfer of medical images is a crucial task and compression algorithms play an inevitable role in generating fruitful solutions [3].

The compression algorithms in general are grouped into two categories; lossy and lossless. The characteristics of lossy and lossless algorithms are as follows; for lossy algorithms, the compression ratio is high and there will be a minimal loss in the reconstructed image quality, for lossless algorithms, there is no change in the quality of decoded image quality when related with the input images, however, the compression ratio is low [4]. A generic classification of lossless image compression schemes are depicted in Figure 1.

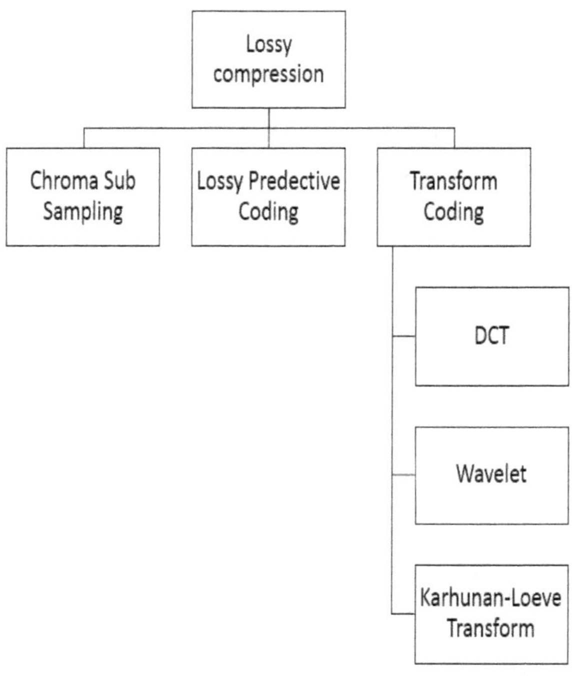

Figure 1. A generic classification lossless image compression techniques.

In general, the lossy compression schemes are classified into two types. They are:

- Entropy coding
- Predictive coding

The predictive coding techniaues are further classified into three categories. They are:

- Gradient adjusted predictor (GAP)
- Median edge detection (MED)
- Gradient edge detection (GED)

The lempel–ziv–welch (LZW) and run length coding (RLE) are the widely used entropy coder in many image compression techniques. The Figure 2 depicts the general classification of lossy compression techniques.

The transform coding is widely used in many image processing applications, the mathematical transform is deployed so that input image is transformed into frequency domain.

The discrete cosine transform (DCT) and discrete wavelet transform (DWT) are the conventional transforms and many variants are there by modifying the classical transforms such as improved DCT, integer wavelet and dual tree complex wavelet techniques.

In most medical field applications, lossless algorithms are used, however, lossy algorithms are used, when a high compression ratio is a requirement [5][6].

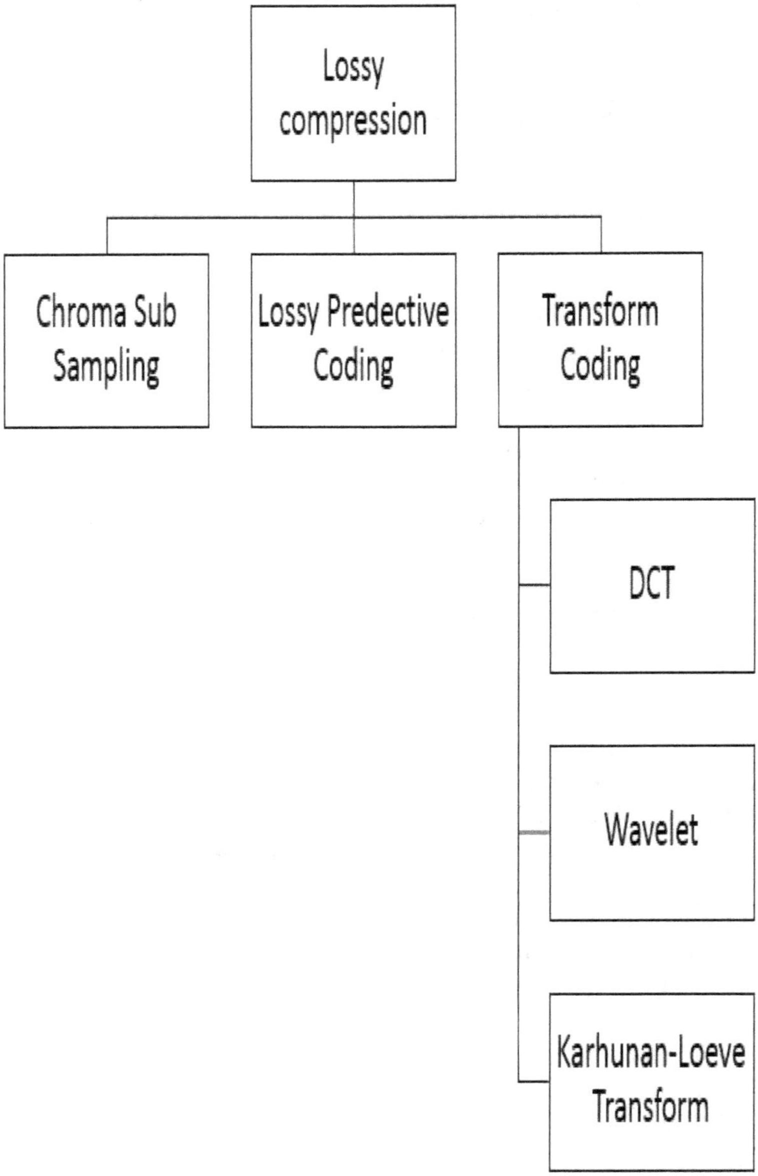

Figure 2. A generic classification lossy image compression techniques.

The chapter organization is as follows:

- Section 2 discusses the different transform domain approaches for compression
- A qualitative analysis of few compression schemes are also highlighted
- Section 3 details the conclusion.

2. Medical image compression using transform domain approaches

The foremost encounter in telemedicine is the storage and transmission of huge size data sets. The tetrolet transform was suggested in [7] for the lossless compression of images. For medical Computed Tomography (CT)/ Magnetic Resonance (MR) images, the compression ratio was in the range of 4 to 4.5, the computational complexity is also low. The tetrolet transform-based image compression works well with noisy images too [7].

A meta-heuristic technique, the game theory approach was coupled with the Finite Impulse Response filter for the medical images. The three phases are:

- Game theory-based compression
- Finite (FIR) filtering
- Error estimation

The compression ratio was high with high peak to signal noise ratio (PSNR) and low mean square error (MSE) when compared with the classical lossy and lossless compression techniques [7].

The lossless compression technique is proposed in this work and the filters have used to improve the quality of the images by eliminating errors, noises, reducing redundancy and recover most of the information in the original image [8]. Figure 3 depicts the 1D and 2D wavelet representation.

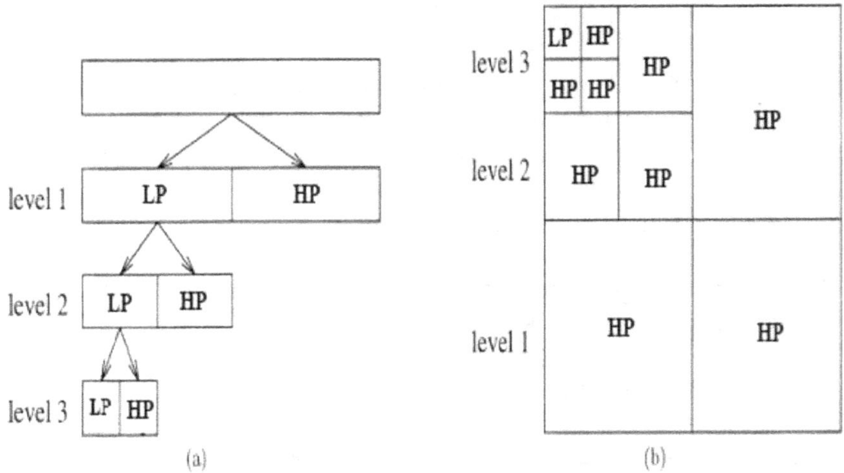

Figure 3. 1D and 2D wavelet representation.

A new framework, comprising of multiscale transforms with encryption/decryption for medical images was proposed in [9]. The input medical image was subjected to bandelet transform and the coefficients are encrypted using the Rivest–Shamir–Adleman (RSA) algorithm.

For encoding, embedded zerotree wavelet (EZW), set partioning in hierarchial trees(SPIHT) , Wavelet Difference Reduction (WDR) and Adaptively Scanned Wavelet Difference Reduction (ASWDR) techniques are used; SPIHT and ASWDR produce proficient results in terms of high PSNR and low MSE, the edge preservation is superior with low computational complexity though encryption is also involved [9].

The wavelet transform coefficients generated are normalized, prediction is done in [10]. The Region of interest (ROI) and non-region of interest (NROI) are extracted before compression. The normalization before prediction improves the accuracy and the predicted coefficients using the masking technique is encoded by an arithmetic coder. The compression scheme proposed in [10] yields proficient results when compared with the JPEG 2000 and other contextual techniques. The ROI is compressed with a high bit rate and NROI is compressed with a low bit rate.

In [11], wavelet transform was employed for the compression of a 3D volumetric data set. The 3D SPIHT algorithm was proposed in [11], because of the high-frequency components, the PSNR value is high and MSE is low for the 3D compression. The results were found to be superior when compared with the compression of 2D images.

A hybrid transform-based image compression comprising of Discrete Wavelet Transform (DWT) and Discrete Cosine Transform (DCT) was employed in [12] for the compression of images. The wavelet transform is applied initially to the medical images and the DCT was applied to LH and HL components.

The DWT and DCT coefficients are subjected to differential pulse code modulation (DPCM) and variable shift coding is applied to generate the compressed data stream. Figure 4 depicts the wavelet and JPEG compression model.

Various methods to improve the performance of the JPEG 2000 algorithm was investigated in [13]. The JP3D algorithm was proposed in [13] for volumetric medical image compression.

At a low bit rate, the classical JPEG 2000 (2D) technique is not proficient in image quality, but the JP3D generates superior image quality. A hybrid compression technique comprising of 2D-Discrete Fractional Fourier Transform and SPIHT algorithm was proposed in [14] for the medical images.

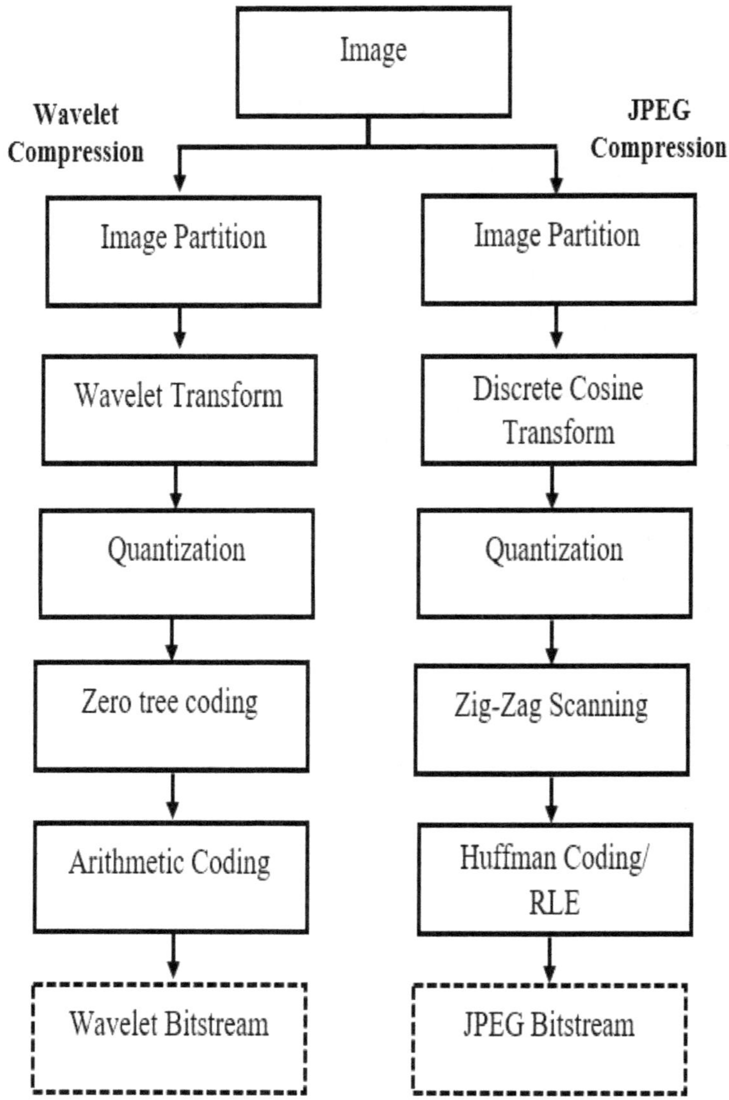

Figure 4. Wavelet and JPEG compression.

The hybrid combination yields a high PSNR value when compared with other classical approaches. The wavelet transform based on the lifting technique was coupled with the SPIHT algorithm was utilized for the medical image compression. The outcomes were found to be efficient when compared with the traditional compression schemes [15].

The different types of wavelets are used for the compression of medical images, the Coiflet wavelet generates high PSNR, and however, the compression ratio is low. The Coiflet wavelet can be utilized in the SPIHT algorithm to generate efficient results [16].

Table 1. Qualitative analysis of compression schemes (T1)

Ref No	Author details	Algorithms used	Source of Data	Inferences
[8]	Li L et al	Game Optimization with fast fourier transform (FFT)	Ultrasound and MR images	PSNR: 65.33 dB and compression ratio 8.91 Robust results, when compared with the JPEG, 3D-DCT and SR-DWT algorithms
[9]	Raja SP	Multiscale transforms	CT, MR and mammogram images	For CT images, PSNR: 54.26 (SPIHT algorithm) For MR images, PSNR:54.47 (SPIHT algorithm) For Mammogram images, PSNR: 54.71 (SPIHT algorithm)
[10]	Eben Sophia P, Anitha J	Wavelet transform with prediction	Benchmark and MR, US images	High PSNR values, when compared with the JPEG algorithm
[11]	Ravichandran D, Ahamad MG, Dhivakar MA	3D SPIHT	3D medical data set	Efficient for volumetric data set, for entropy coding, Huffman coder was used
[12]	Yadav V, Verma M, Kaushik VD	DWT and DCT	US and X-ray images	For performance comparison, JPEG algorithm was used PSNR> 30dB

[13]	Bruylants T, Munteanu A, Schelkens P	JP3D	3D medical data set	Proficient results, when compared with the H.265/HEVC and JPEG algorithms
[14]	Kumari PV, Thanushkodi K	Hybrid compression model comprising of 2D discrete fractional Fourier transform	CT images of lungs	PSNR value of 40.90dB was obtained and superior results, when compared with the classical compression approaches
[15]	Kabir MA et al	Lifting based wavelet transform with SPIHT	MR images of the brain	PSNR>25 dB, produces efficient results when compared with the classical SPIHT and EZW schemes

A comparative analysis of medical image compression using wavelet and contourlet transform was put forward in [17]. The performance of DWT was found to be superior for low compression ratio, however, for high compression ratio, the performance of contourlet transform was found to be good.

In [18], a detailed study on medical image compression and its need is highlighted, the features of lossy and lossless compression techniques are discussed. The ROI based compression and residual techniques gain prominence. The basic features of ROI based compression for 2D images, volumetric data set and medical videos are described in [19].

The ROI based compression was found to be useful for teleradiology application for disease diagnosis. A hybrid compression technique comprising of DCT sub-band decomposition with an improved SPIHT algorithm was proposed for medical images. The improved SPIHT algorithm focus on the insignificant coefficients of DCT that represents the high-frequency components [20].

The DCT with adaptive threshold value was employed in [21] for the classification of blocks in the compression model. The adaptive thresholding improves the superiority of the reconstructed image. The embedded set partitioning significant and zero block coding were highlighted in [22] for the compression of medical images, it was formulated from set partitioning embedded block.

The distortion observed was low, when compared with the classical algorithms. The adaptive prediction was incorporated in the wavelet compression scheme to improve the accuracy. The adaptive prediction overcomes the multicollinearity problem, generates a high compression ratio when compared with the classical methods [23].

The selection of appropriate wavelet for medical image compression was proposed in [24], the biorthogonal wavelet was found to be proficient when compared with the classical methods. Figure 5 depicts the ROI based wavelet transformation.

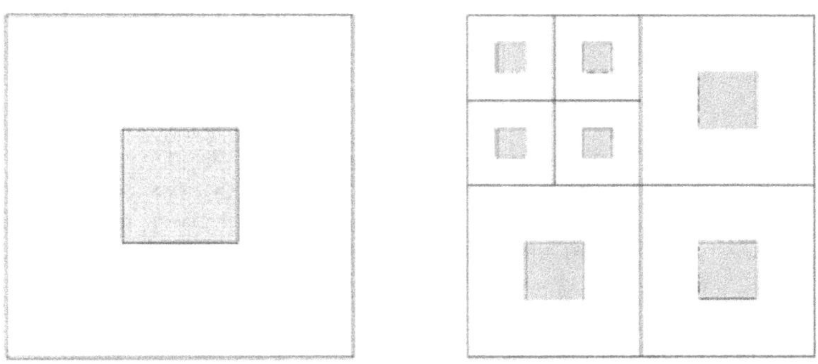

(a) (b)

Figure 5. ROI based wavelet transformation.

A hybrid medical image compression scheme comprising of DWT and DCT was highlighted in [25]. The results were found to be superior when compared with the SPIHT and JPEG coder. The wavelet transform was found to be proficient for the lossy and lossless compression technique.

The article [26] highlights the ROI based compression using wavelet and can be used for mobile application. The 3D DCT was employed in

[27] for the compression of medical images, Huffman coding was utilized for entropy coding. Tables 1, 2 and 3 represents qualitative analysis of compression schemes.

The PSNR, MSE and compression ratio are the widely used metrics for the validation of compression techniques. High value of PSNR and low value of MSE is a good indicator of a proficient compression technique. The compression ratio relies on the type of compression, for lossy techniaues, the compression ratio will be high and for lossless technique, the compression ratio is low.

Table 2. Qualitative analysis of compression schemes

Ref No	Author Details	Algorithms used	Source of Data	Inferences
[17]	Riazifar N, Yazdi M	Wavelet and contourlet transform	CT images	PSNR>32 dB (for low CR) (Wavelet transform) PSNR>35 db (for high CR) (contourlet transform) Edge preservation is better in contourlet transform
[20]	Chen YY	DCT with Improved SPIHT	Angiogram, Ultrasound and Lena images	Produces superior results, when compared with the SPIHT and JPEG 2000 techniques PSNR values of DCT-Improved SPIHT for 0.15, 0.37, 0.80 and 2 are 37.2, 39.8, 43.6 and 50
[21]	Singh S, Kumar V, Verma HK	DCT with adaptive thresholding	CT, X-ray and Ultrasound images	Mean PSNR >24 and proficient results, when related with the JPEG compression model
[22]	Palanisamy G, Samukutti A	Embedded set partitioning significant and zero block	Medical and standard database images	Average PSNR>30 dB Competent results, when related with the

		coding (ESPSZBC)		SPIHT and set partitioning embedded block (SPECK) coders
[23]	Chen YT, Tseng DC	Wavelet transform with adaptive prediction	CT, MR and Ultrasound images	The compression rate was 20.7, 12.6, 8.02, and 3.47% for SPIHT, JPEG2000, CALIC, and SSM methods respectively.
[25]	Singh S, Kumar V, Verma HK	Hybrid compression comprising of DCT and DWT	CT, Ultrasound and X-ray images	PSNR > 31dB (CT images) PSNR> 27dB (US images) PSNR>32 dB(X-ray images) Efficient results when compared with SPIHT and JPEG algorithms
[27]	Raj VN, Venkateswarlu T	3D DCT	X-ray images	Proficient results were produced when compared with the JPEG algorithm PSNR: 41.65 with bpp: 0.67
[28]	Ansari MA, Anand RS	Wavelet transform	CT images of chest and brain	PSNR: 24dB(chest images) PSNR: 22 to 34 dB (brain images)

The wavelet transform coefficients are subjected to a biorthogonal filter bank and the SPIHT algorithm is utilized in [29] for compression. The integer wavelet transform with predictive encoding/decoding was suggested in [30] for the compression.

The prediction based transform domain approach yield proficient results, when compared with the classical techniques. A hybrid combination of DCT and fractal image compression was utilized in [31] for the compression. Superior results were produced, when compared with the classical methods in terms of the performance metrics for the benchmark images.

The DCT was coupled with the adaptive block scanning for the compression of colour images [32]. The colour images in RGB format was converted into YCbCr format and for entropy coding, a Huffman coder was employed [32].

Table 3. Qualitative analysis of compression schemes (T3)

Ref No	Author Details	Algorithm Used	Source of Data	Inferences
[33]	Bruckmann A, Uhl A	SPIHT with biorthogonal filter bank	CT, MR and US images	PSNR > than 40dB and proficient results were produced, when compared with the JPEG and EZQ algorithms
[34]	Shih FY, Wu YT	DCT and genetic algorithm	MR images	PSNR> 35dB and produces robust results when compared with the classical compression algorithms
[38]	Dilmaghani RS et al	EZW algorithm	MR and mammogram images	Performance was found to be superior when compared with the JPEG algorithm. PSNR>25dB with a high compression ratio
[39]	Zhu Z et al	JPEG	COVID 19 CT images	The classification was found to be proficient using deep learning with the compression technique
[40]	Haouari B	Quincunx wavelet coupled with SPIHT	3D medical dataset	Efficient results were produced in terms of the PSNR and structural similarity index.

The ROI based compression yield prominence for telemedicine applications and in [33], the features of the direct and residual region of interest coding are discussed. The DCT was utilized in the watermarking and compression of medical images; the genetic algorithm was employed for the optimum selection of coefficients [34].

The DWT with bitplane approach was employed in [35] for the compression and it relies on ROI [35]. The multiple array technique was employed in [36] for the compression of medical images, lossy and lossless algorithms are discussed and the multiple array technique was found to be proficient for telemedicine application.

A comparative analysis of JPEG and JPEG 2000 was projected in [37] for compression, the JPEG 2000 results are superior when related to the JPEG algorithm. The embedded zero tree wavelet algorithm was proposed in [38] for the compression of medical images and the results were found to be superior when compared with the JPEG algorithm.

A variation of wavelet transform Quincunx wavelet was coupled with SPIHT for the compression of the 3D data set, the results were robust when compared with the classical approaches [39]. The compressed CT images of the chest by JPEG algorithm was utilized in the classification of COVID 19 using a deep learning algorithm [40].

3. Benefits of medical image compression and its role in telemedicine

The DICOM images are superior quality images and needs high bandwidth for data storage and transmission. The medical image compression gains prominence in minimizing the file size for medical data storage and transfer, gains importance in picture archiving and communication systems (PACS).The medical image compression minimizes the storage and transmission cost by deploying lossy and lossless algorithms [41].

The JPEG lossy compression model was found to be proficient for the compression of X-ray and other color medical images [42]. A detailed study of lossy compression techniques for the PACS was highlighted in [43].

The image compression standards and its features for telemedicine application are highlighted in [44]. The orthogonal and wavelet transform based compression was found to be proficient, when compared with the classical techniques. The Huffman coder was found to be robust, when compared with the JPEG 2000 in terms of computational complexity and other performance metrics for medical images compression [45].

The performance metrics for the assessment of compression techniques for medical images are put forward in [46]. The 3D SPIHT algorithm yields proficient results for the compression of color DICOM images [47].

The telemedicine utilizes the intetnet connectivity to transfer the images from one node to another node. The compression model aids telemedicine in data storage and transfer. The characterstics of wireless telemedicine system was highlighted in [48].

The ROI based compression was highlighted in [49] for telemedicine application, the integer wavelet transform exhibits superior reconstruction image quality. The legendary moments coupled with whale optimization technique find its application in compression of medical images for telemedicine application [50]. The adaptive prediction techniques for medical image/video compression is highlighted in [51].

The following inferences are made from this research work

- Compression plays vital role in reducing the file size , paves the way for big data handling storage and display
- Compression algorithm is not unique and it varies with respect to the medical imaging modality
- Compression algorithms are validated by performance metrics and the quality of reconstructed image is vital for physicians and radiologist for disease diagnosis and treatment planning
- Lossy compression models are also preferred for medical images subjected to the constrain in the validation of reconstructed image quality
- Parameter tuning palce crucial role in compression techniques and optimization algorithms are deployed for optimum tuning of parameters
- Reconstructed image quality is a vital factor, how ever the compression ratio and computational complexity have to be also considered in the real time scenario especially for telemediciene application

- Compression algorithms aids the telemedicine in viewing and analyzing images through mobile based applications too.
- For hardware implementation of compression algorithm, choice of embedded processor is vital and the private cloud network is utilized for data staorage and transfer

3. Conclusion

This chapter proposes an exclusive analysis of transform domain approaches for medical image compression. The classical transform domain approaches and the improved versions of classical techniques are discussed in this work.

Few hybrid compression approaches are also highlighted in this work. There is no universal algorithm for the compression of images, the performance of algorithms changes with respect to the medical imaging modality and its characteristics.

There is evidence that lossy techniques can also be used for medical images when the reconstructed image quality is good and validated by metrics. The outcome of this work can be useful to focus on transform domain approaches for medical image compression. The need for efficient compression is vital since digital data storage and transfer is gaining prominence in this current pandemic scenario for telemedicine applications.

Acknowledgement

The authors would like to acknowledge the support from the Schmitt Center for Biomedical Instrumentation (SCBMI) of Amal Jyothi College of Engineering for supporting this work.

References

1. Van den Branden Lambrecht, C. J. (2013). *Vision models and applications to image and video processing.* Ist Volume, First edition, Springer Science & Business Media.
2. Mustra, M., Delac, K., & Grgic, M. (2008, September). Overview of the DICOM standard. In *2008 50th International Symposium ELMAR* (Vol. 1, pp. 39-44). IEEE.

3. Dougherty, G. (Ed.). (2011). *Medical image processing: techniques and applications.* Ist Volume, First edition , Springer Science & Business Media.
4. Vijayvargiya, G., Silakari, S., & Pandey, R. (2013). A survey: various techniques of image compression. *arXiv preprint arXiv:1311.6877.*
5. McAuliffe, M. J., Lalonde, F. M., McGarry, D., Gandler, W., Csaky, K., & Trus, B. L. (2001, July). Medical image processing, analysis and visualization in clinical research. In *Proceedings 14th IEEE Symposium on Computer-Based Medical Systems. CBMS 2001* (pp. 381-386). IEEE.
6. Menegaz G. (2006). Trends in medical image compression. Current Medical Imaging.,2(2),pp.165-85
7. UmaMaheswari S, SrinivasaRaghavan V. (2021) Lossless medical image compression algorithm using tetrolet transformation. Journal of Ambient Intelligence and Humanized Computing. 12(3):pp.4127-35.
8. Li L, Muneeswaran V, Ramkumar S, Emayavaramban G, Gonzalez GR.(2019), Metaheuristic FIR filter with game theory based compression technique-A reliable medical image compression technique for online applications. Pattern Recognition Letters.125, pp.7-12.
9. Raja SP. (2019). Joint medical image compression–encryption in the cloud using multiscale transform-based image compression encoding techniques. Sādhanā.;44(2).pp.28.
10. Eben Sophia P, Anitha J.(2017),Contextual medical image compression using normalized wavelet-transform coefficients and prediction. IETE Journal of Research.;63(5),pp.671-83.
11. Ravichandran D, Ahamad MG, Dhivakar MA.(2016),Performance analysis of three-dimensional medical image compression based on discrete wavelet transform. In2016 22nd International Conference on Virtual System & Multimedia (VSMM), IEEE, pp. 1-8.
12. Yadav V, Verma M, Kaushik VD.(2015), A hybrid image compression technique for medical images. International Conference on Computational Intelligence and Communication Networks (CICN) , IEEE. pp. 222-227.
13. Bruylants T, Munteanu A, Schelkens P. (2015), Wavelet based volumetric medical image compression. Signal processing: Image communication. pp. 112-33.
14. Kumari PV, Thanushkodi K. (2013), A secure fast 2D—Discrete fractional fourier transform based medical image compression using hybrid encoding technique.International conference on current trends in engineering and technology (ICCTET), IEEE, pp. 1-7
15. Kabir MA, Khan MM, Islam MT, Hossain ML, Mitul AF.(2013) Image compression using lifting based wavelet transform coupled with SPIHT algorithm.International Conference on Informatics, Electronics and Vision (ICIEV), IEEE. pp. 1-4
16. Gopi K, Shri TR.(2013),Medical image compression using wavelets. IOSR Journal of VLSI and signal processing (IOSR-JVSP) ,2(4),pp.1-6.

17. Riazifar N, Yazdi M. (2009), Effectiveness of contourlet vs wavelet transform on medical image compression: a comparative study. World Academy of Science, Engineering and Technology. ,49(3):pp.837-42.
18. Zukoski MJ, Boult T, Iyriboz T.(2006) A novel approach to medical image compression. International journal of bioinformatics research and applications.2(1),pp.89-103.
19. Doukas C, Maglogiannis I. (2007), Region of interest coding techniques for medical image compression. IEEE Engineering in medicine and Biology Magazine.26(5),pp.29-35.
20. Chen YY.(2007), Medical image compression using DCT-based subband decomposition and modified SPIHT data organization. International journal of medical informatics.76(10),pp.717-25.
21. Singh S, Kumar V, Verma HK.(2007),Adaptive threshold-based block classification in medical image compression for teleradiology. Computers in Biology and Medicine.37(6),pp.811-9.
22. Palanisamy G, Samukutti A.(2008),Medical image compression using a novel embedded set partitioning significant and zero block coding. Int. Arab J. Inf. Technol.5(2),pp.132-9.
23. Chen YT, Tseng DC.(2007),Wavelet-based medical image compression with adaptive prediction. Computerized medical Imaging and graphics.31(1),pp.1-8.
24. Bairagi VK, Sapkal AM.(2009),Selection of wavelets for medical image compression. International Conference on Advances in Computing, Control, and Telecommunication Technologies, IEEE, pp.678-680
25. Singh S, Kumar V, Verma HK.(2007), DWT–DCT hybrid scheme for medical image compression. Journal of medical engineering & technology,31(2),pp.109-22.
26. Doukas CN, Maglogiannis I, Kormentzas G.(2005), Medical image compression using wavelet transform on mobile devices with ROI coding support. IEEE Engineering in Medicine and Biology 27th Annual Conference,pp.3779-3784
27. Raj VN, Venkateswarlu T.(2007), A novel approach to medical image compression using sequential 3D DCT. InInternational Conference on Computational Intelligence and Multimedia Applications (ICCIMA 2007),Vol. 3, IEEE. pp.146-152
28. Ansari MA, Anand RS.(2009), Comparative analysis of medical image compression techniques and their performance evaluation for telemedicine. Proc. International Conference on Cognition and Recognition ,pp. 670-677
29. Anju B, Manimurugan S.(2012), An approach to medical image compression using filters based on lifting scheme. IOSR Journal of VLSI and Signal Processing.1(2),pp.9-16.
30. Shirsat TG, Bairagi VK.(2013), Lossless medical image compression by IWT and predictive coding. International Conference on Energy Efficient Technologies for Sustainability,IEEE,pp.1279-1283.

31. Rawat C, Meher S.(2013),A Hybrid Image Compression Scheme Using DCT and Fractal Image Compression. Int. Arab J. Inf. Technol,10(6),pp.553-62.
32. Douak F, Benzid R, Benoudjit N.(2011),Color image compression algorithm based on the DCT transform combined to an adaptive block scanning. AEU-International Journal of Electronics and Communications.65(1),pp.16-26.
33. Bruckmann A, Uhl A.(2000). Selective medical image compression techniques for telemedical and archiving applications. Computers in biology and medicine.30(3),pp.153-69.
34. Shih FY, Wu YT.(2005),Robust watermarking and compression for medical images based on genetic algorithms. Information Sciences.175(3),pp.200-16.
35. Lee HK, Kim HJ, Kwon KR, Lee JK.(2005), ROI medical image watermarking using DWT and bit-plane. Asia-Pacific Conference on Communications, IEEE, pp. 512-515.
36. Devaraj K, Munukur RK, Kesavamurthy T.(2005), Lossless medical-image compression using multiple array technique.International Symposium on Intelligent Signal Processing and Communication Systems IEEE, pp. 837-840.
37. OH TH, Besar R.(2002),Medical image compression using JPEG-2000 and JPEG: A comparison study. Journal of Mechanics in Medicine and Biology,pp.313-28.
38. Dilmaghani RS, Ahmadian A, Ghavami M, Aghvami AH.(2004),Progressive medical image transmission and compression. IEEE signal processing letters.11(10),pp.806-9.
39. Zhu Z, Xingming Z, Tao G, Dan T, Li J, Chen X, Li Y, Zhou Z, Zhang X, Zhou J, Chen D.(2021), Classification of COVID-19 by compressed chest CT image through deep learning on a large patients cohort. Interdisciplinary Sciences: Computational Life Sciences.13(1),pp.73-82.
40. Haouari B.(2020),3D Medical image compression using the quincunx wavelet coupled with SPIHT. Indonesian J. Electric Eng. Comput. Science, 18:821.
41. Nasıfoğlu, Hüseyin, and Osman Eroğul.(2019),"Medical Image Compression for Telemedicine Applications." , Archives in Biomedical Engineering & Biotechnology
42. Kajiwara KI.(1992),JPEG compression for PACS. Computer methods and programs in biomedicine.37(4),pp.343-51.
43. Dragan D, Ivetic D.(2009),A comprehensive quality evaluation system for PACS. InUbiquitous Computing and Communication Journal, Special Issue on ICIT 2009 Conference-Bioinformatics and Image,Vol. 4, No. 3, pp. 642-650.
44. Wilson DL.(1995),Image compression requirements and standards in PACS.Medical Imaging PACS Design and Evaluation: Engineering and Clinical Issues,Vol. 2435, pp. 564-572. International Society for Optics and Photonics.

45. Rahmat RF, Andreas TS, Fahmi F, Pasha MF, Alzahrani MY, Budiarto R.(2019),Analysis of dicom image compression alternative using huffman coding. Journal of healthcare engineering.
46. Kocsis O, Costaridou L, Mandellos G, Lymberopoulos D, Panayiotakis G.(2003),Compression assessment based on medical image quality concepts using computer-generated test images. Computer methods and programs in biomedicine.71(2),pp.105-15.
47. Kesavamurthy T, Rani S. (2008),Dicom color medical image compression using 3D-SPIHT for pacs application. International journal of biomedical science,4(2),pp.113.
48. Pattichis CS, Kyriacou E, Voskarides S, Pattichis MS, Istepanian R, Schizas CN.(2002),Wireless telemedicine systems: an overview. IEEE Antennas and Propagation Magazine.44(2),pp.143-53.
49. Bairagi VK, Sapkal AM.(2013), ROI-based DICOM image compression for telemedicine. Sadhana. 38(1),pp.123-31.
50. Hosny KM, Khalid AM, Mohamed ER.(2021),Optimized medical image compression for telemedicine applications. InArtificial Intelligence and Data Mining in Healthcare,Springer, Cham, pp. 119-142
51. Pathak KC, Sarvaiya JN, Darji AD.(2019),Adaptive prediction methods for medical image/video compression for telemedicine application. InHistopathological Image Analysis in Medical Decision Making, IGI Global,pp. 244-275.

9

Advances in Healthcare Sector

Divya Kalra and Shikha Goyal

Lovely Professional University, Phagwara, Punjab, India

Abstract

With advancements in technology, the world is transforming greatly. Through technology and innovation, the world has transformed greatly in such a way that different things like medicines, video consultation from doctors, etc. are just a few clicks away. Keeping the organizations updated with the newer methods of working is pushing the world to get closer and connected to each other. Different technologies and their modern methods are bringing advances in healthcare sector and making the work easier. In this chapter, the different advances in healthcare sector which are seen in the form of telemedicine, application of chatbot, etc. that are being used are discussed. Along with this, the advantages and disadvantages that different advances have in healthcare sector are discussed and stated.

1. Introduction

Healthcare sector is undoubtedly one of the most crucial and important sectors. Health of every individual is very important. Healthcare sector always carries great responsibility of the society. This sector keeps on progressing and updating in accordance with the advancements in technology. So, there have been a lot of advances in healthcare sector. Some examples of the advances in healthcare sector are explained further on in this chapter.

2. Advances in healthcare sector

Any technology that can truly help the doctors, medical staff and patients in a proven way will be considered beneficial. Technology is used in all sectors, for example, be it education sector or healthcare sector or financial sector, etc. the usage of technology is present everywhere.

One of the biggest advantage of technology is it helps in making work simpler and easier. Depending upon the type of technology, there are various applications of it in different sectors.

In healthcare sector various technologies have brought about advances in this sector. In the next section, the examples of the advances in healthcare sector are explained.

3. Examples of advances in healthcare sector

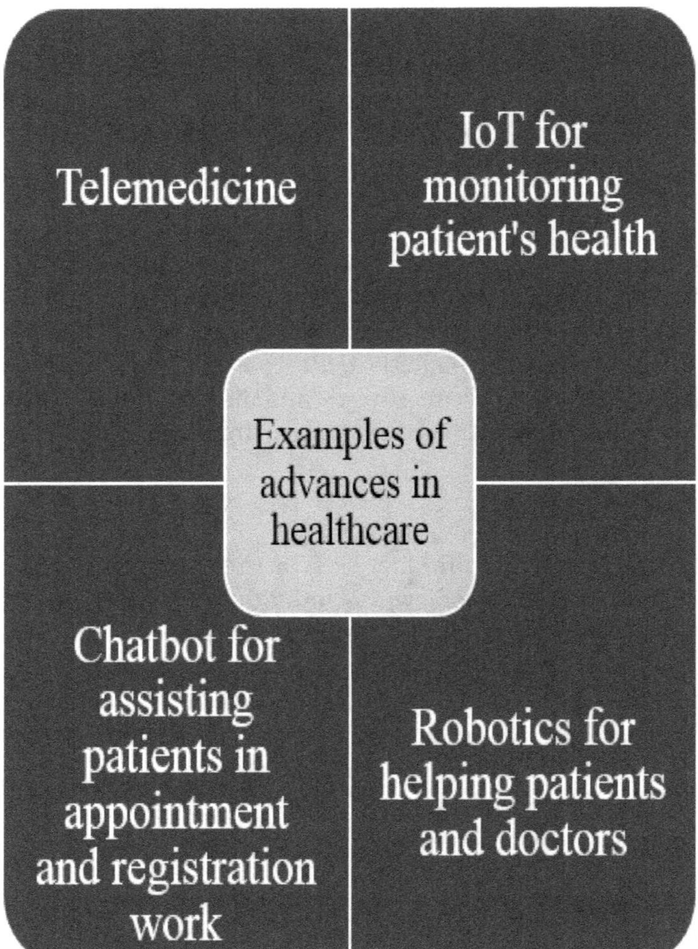

Figure 1. Examples of advances in healthcare sector.

There are many examples of advances in healthcare. In this chapter, some examples of advances in healthcare will be discussed. Those examples are shown in Figure 1.

3.1 Telemedicine

Telemedicine in simple terms is usage of telecommunication technologies to provide remote healthcare services and treatment to patients. The patients can take consultation from doctors using telecommunication services like call, video, text, message and the doctors can also do diagnosis and treatment of their patients. Telemedicine is useful in various cases. Below are some examples where telemedicine can be useful:

- When patients are unable to personally visit the doctor: In cases where the patients are unable to themselves go and visit the doctor be it due to any reason, in such cases telemedicine can be extremely useful for the patients.
- In condition like pandemic, telemedicine is a great option: Pandemic like Covid19 where maintaining social distancing is one of the top priorities, the option of telemedicine can be reliable. It can be the instant go to option when in need of healthcare services and treatment.
- When there is extreme urgency: At times when there is extreme urgency and the patient requires immediate help from the doctor, telemedicine can be useful.

In the case of pandemic or even in the case when pandemic is not there, telemedicine is truly a great resource. It is one of the advantageous advances of healthcare sector. It benefits the patients and also makes the work of the doctors little easier.

During pandemic the utilization of telemedicine option has increased. Owing to the restrictions in pandemic of lockdown and social distancing, telemedicine proved to be a great option and also a great relief in case of urgency of reaching out to the doctor.

There will be cases when people need to visit doctor in person for treatment where telemedicine will not be sufficient enough to help the patients which is a drawback but still telemedicine can in help following up with the doctor later on.

Leaving this drawback apart, there are various advantages of telemedicine which are beneficial for everyone. Figure 2 below shows various advantages of telemedicine.

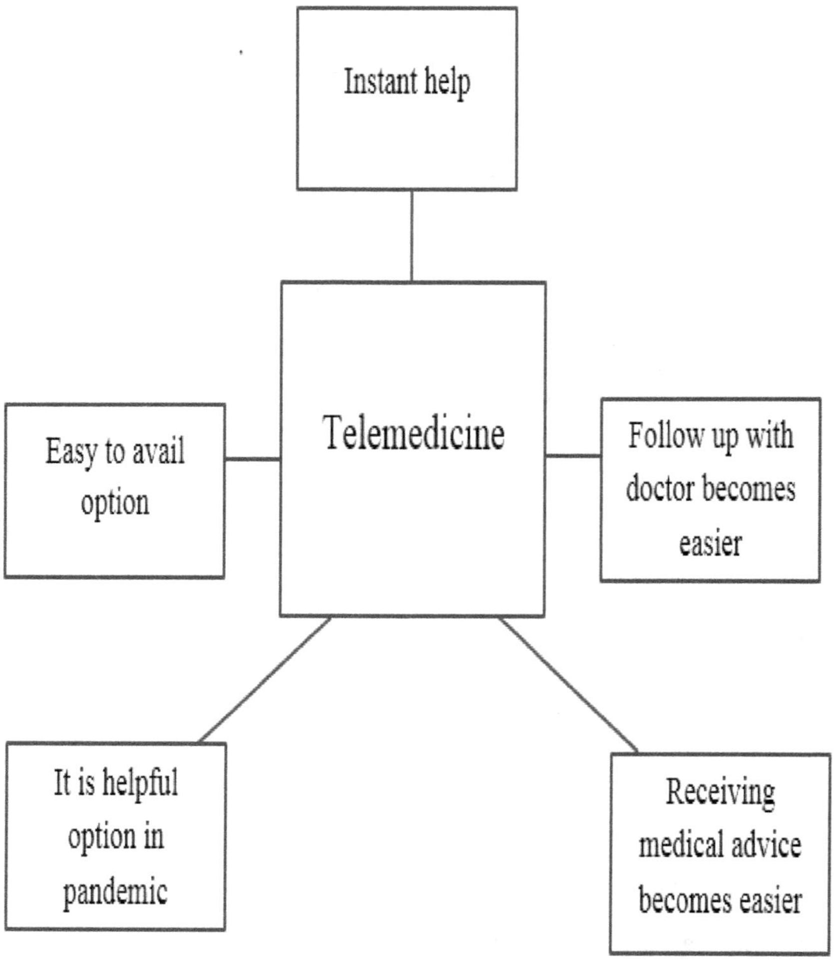

Figure 2. Advantages of telemedicine.

Advantages of Telemedicine in healthcare sector

There are several advantages of telemedicine in healthcare sector. They are as follows:

- Instant help: Telemedicine helps in receiving instant help in healthcare matters from doctors. The patients can reach out to the doctors regarding their healthcare matters and receive instant help via telemedicine.
- Easy to avail option: It is an easy to avail option in healthcare matters in emergency. Whenever there is any emergency, telemedicine becomes the one of the easiest to avail options for the patients.
- Follow up with doctor becomes easier: Through telemedicine, it is easier for the patients to follow up with the doctor regarding their health.
- Receiving medical advice becomes easier: It makes receiving medical help and advice very easier and convenient as the patients can receive them at any moment and from any place.
- It is helpful option in pandemic: Telemedicine is a great option in times of pandemic where it is difficult to visit the doctor personally for healthcare matters. In extreme serious health condition where patient has to visit the hospital for treatment then telemedicine would not be very helpful as discussed and mentioned earlier but in cases where visiting the hospital can be avoided, telemedicine will be a great option indeed.

Thus, overall if one views telemedicine then it will seem to be having following features:

- Great potential
- User friendly
- Advantageous
- Extremely helpful

Thus, telemedicine overall is very useful. It is one of great advances in healthcare sector.

3.2 Internet of things (IOT) for monitoring patient's health

IoT can be used in healthcare for monitoring patient's health. IoT is useful in keeping connectivity between objects or devices. IoT helps in keeping things connected through internet.

In healthcare, IoT can be used in keeping patients connected with doctors. When in certain condition patients are in need of constant tracking of their health, IoT can help in keeping track of patient's health and monitoring it.

Consider the following example case where IoT in healthcare can be useful.

When any patient's heart rate needs to be monitored constantly, then in such cases IoT can be helpful. Even without the doctor being in front of the patient, IoT can help in monitoring patient's heart rate constantly. The functions IoT can perform in this example case are:

- IoT can help in updating the doctor regarding the patient's health condition regularly and keep the patient connected with doctor.
- IoT can help in sending regular updates of patient's heart rate to doctor and also when there is some abnormality in the heart rate of the patient, it can notify the doctor. This will help both the doctor and the patient.
- Heart rate monitoring sensor will keep on gathering the heart rate data and the processed heart data will be sent to the doctor through IoT. The doctor can then easily keep on monitoring the patient's heart rate as the doctor will keep on receiving real time updates of the heart rate.

In case there is sudden abnormality in heart, the doctor in this case will be sent special notification. From above example, it is clear that IoT is very useful in healthcare for monitoring patient's condition.

This above example can be even understood with the help of the diagram shown below in Figure 3.

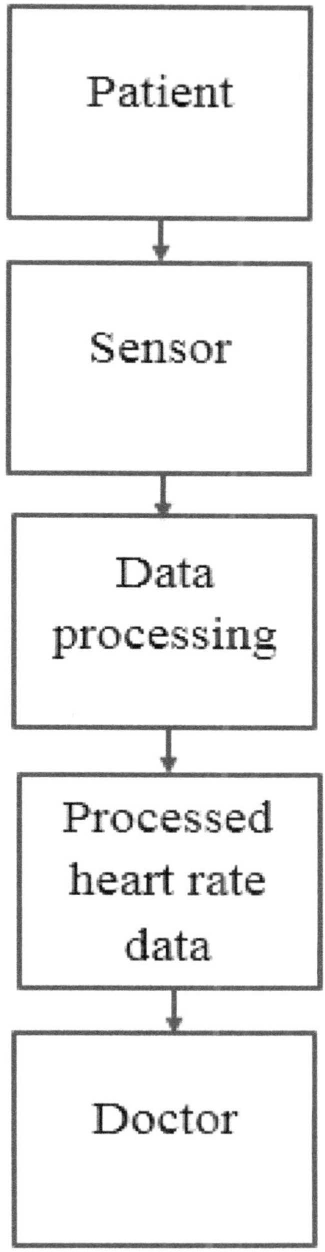

Figure 3. Working process of IoT in heart rate monitoring of patient.

The working process of the example is as follows:

- Patient: The patient will have the sensor setup attached to him/her.
- Sensor: The sensor setup will gather heart rate data.
- Data Processing: The gathered heart rate data will be sent for processing.
- Processed Heart Rate Data: The processed data will be sent to the doctor.
- Doctor: The doctor will keep on receiving the heart rate data of the patient.

IoT can thus help in monitoring patients. It can thus help in patient's healthcare.

Advantages of IoT for monitoring patient's health

- IoT can keep doctor and patient virtually connected regarding patient's health.
- Despite of the patient not being in front of the doctor, the patient's health can be monitored (In the case of heart rate monitoring example explained above, the patient's heart rate can be monitored by the doctor without being in front of the patient.)
- In the case of some abnormality observed in health of the patient, doctor will be notified immediately (In the case of heart rate monitoring example explained above, when there is some abnormality in the heart rate, the doctor will be notified).
- Doctor can keep on receiving real time updates on patient's health condition. (In the case of heart rate monitoring example explained above, the doctor will receive real time updates of the heart rate of the patient).

3.3 Chatbot for assisting patients in appointment and registration work

Chatbot is applicable at many places. From corporate sector to healthcare sector, chatbot is often used. In healthcare sector, it can help patients in appointment and registration work.

A chatbot is a type of conversational agent, a computer program basically designed to have a conversation with humans in natural language via text or audio methods. In short, it is an assistant who exists virtually.

It is programmed to automatically answer user's request. It basically supports the users by answering their questions. It provides immediate answers and is available mostly always.

In healthcare sector, for instance, as mentioned above, chatbots are most commonly used in registration or appointment-based chats done by the patients wherein there are pre decided answers or programmed answers based on the information it is fed with.

On the basis of the fed or programmed information, it just provides a quick response to all the patients thereby helping them, and thus even reducing the workload of doctors and their team.

Advantages of chatbot for assisting patients in appointment and registration work

- Chatbot can be available all throughout the day.
- Chatbot can instantly reply and help patients with registration related questions.
- Chatbot can instantly reply and help patients with appointment related questions.
- Chatbot can reduce workload of doctors and their team by quickly responding patients about registration or appointment related queries.

3.4 Robotics for helping patients and doctors

Robotics can help both patients and doctors in healthcare. During pandemic time where social distancing is required, taking help of robots in hospitals can be helpful. Doctors with the help of robots can send food and medicine to patients through them. Doctors can even send some message and remind the patients some healthcare instructions through robot. Except for this, robot can used in assisting doctors in surgeries. Hence if viewed in overall totality, robotics in healthcare can be used helping patients and doctors.

Advantages of robotics for helping patients and doctors

- Robotics can help doctors and patients to quite an extent by going and giving food and medicine to patients especially during pandemic where social distancing is required.
- Doctors can send food and medicine to the patients in hospital through robot.
- Any important healthcare message or healthcare instructions can be sent to patients by doctors through robot.
- Robots can assist in surgeries.

4. Advantages of recent advances in healthcare sector

Today's world is full of technology and innovation, leading to advances in various sectors. The healthcare sector has also experienced many advances and this sector is still continuing becoming advanced. With all the advances, providing quality healthcare to everyone has been the priority and aim. The advances in healthcare sector are resulting in a lot of advantages which are discussed in the chapter for each example of advances in healthcare sector. Below is list of combined summarized advantages from all the examples of advances in healthcare sector. This will help in understanding the comparison with disadvantages of advances in healthcare in sector which will be discussed after the below list.

- Reaching out to doctors and getting consultation, treatment, etc. has become easier with telemedicine option.
- Monitoring of the patient's health becomes convenient and easier with IoT.
- Constant real time updates regarding patient's health can be sent to doctor with IoT.
- Doctor and their team's workload can be reduced when it comes to handling questions related to registration and appointments with chatbots.
- Patients and doctors both can receive healthcare assistance and doctors can receive additional assistance in their work with robotics.

5. Disadvantages of recent advances in healthcare sector

In contrary to the above-mentioned points, recent advances the healthcare sector is bring in disadvantages as well. The above discussed advantages can be compared with disadvantages below. Some of the disadvantages are:

- Data privacy remains to be one of the challenge of the hospital, technology is by and large considered to breach the privacy and security issues
- The huge investment cost involved in the use and execution of technological advances is a burden on the part of the management
- Sometimes, risk and defects are concerned with the technology being used in the hospitals like surgery done with the help of robots etc.

6. Conclusion

Healthcare sector is very important for everyone. There are many advances in healthcare sector. The examples of advances in healthcare sector are explained in this chapter. The advances in the healthcare sector are seen in the form of telemedicine, internet of things (IoT) for monitoring patient's health, etc. These advances have advantages as well as disadvantages. While disadvantages are few, steps should be taken in the direction of eliminating the few disadvantages completely. This will be huge achievement for healthcare sector.

References

[1] Agomo, Chijioke. (2008). Telemedicine improving health services through technology. Pharmaceutical Journal. 281.103-105.

[2] Bagchi S. (2006). Telemedicine in rural India. PLoS medicine, 3(3), e82. https://doi.org/10.1371/journal.pmed.0030082

[3] Ben-Assuli, O. (2015). Electronic health records, adoption, quality of care, legal and privacy issues and their implementation in emergency departments. Health policy, 119(3), 287-297.

[4] Kukafka, R., J. S. Ancker, C. Chan, J. Chelico, S. Khan, S. Mortoti, K. Natarajan, K. Presley, and K. Stephens. 2007. Redesigning electronic health record systems to support public health. *Journal of Biomedical Informatics,* 40 (4):398–409. doi: 10.1016/j.jbi.2007.07.001.

[5] Shen, Y., Guo, D., Long, F., Mateos, L. A., Ding, H., Xiu, Z., Hellman, R. B.,

King, A, Chen, S. Zhang, C. and Tan, H. (2021). Robots Under COVID-19 Pandemic: A Comprehensive Survey. *IEEE Access*. Vol. 9, pp. 1590-1615, doi: 10.1109/ACCESS.2020.3045792.

[6] P. Kandpal, K. Jasnani, R. Raut and S. Bhorge, "Contextual Chatbot for Healthcare Purposes (using Deep Learning)," *2020 Fourth World Conference on Smart Trends in Systems, Security and Sustainability (WorldS4)*, 2020, pp. 625-634, doi: 10.1109/WorldS450073.2020.9210351.

[7] Houssamia, N., Kirkpatrick-Jones, G., Noguchi, N., and Lee, C. (2019) Artificial Intelligence (AI) for the early detection of breast cancer: a scoping review to assess AI's potential in breast screening practice, Expert Review of Medical Devices, 16, 351-362.

[8] Kirtana, R. N., and Lokeswari, Y. V., (2017). An IoT based remote HRV monitoring system for hypertensive patients. *International Conference on Computer, Communication and Signal ProcessinG.* pp. 1-6, doi: 10.1109/ICCCSP.2017.7944086.

[9] Semuil Tjiharjadi & Aufar Fajar (2017). Human Heart Rate Detection Application. *International Conference on Soft Computing, Intelligent System and Information Technology (ICSIIT)*, pp. 167-172, doi: 10.1109/ICSIIT.2017.12.

10

Advantages of Artificial Intelligence in Education and Healthcare Sectors

Anju Asokan

Sri Krishna College of Technology, Kovaipudur, Coimbatore, India

Abstract

Artificial Intelligence (AI) has many advantages in general. In this chapter, the advantages of AI in education sector and healthcare sector are considered. AI can help in healthcare providing data with high precision and accuracy allowing humans to get wider insight into diagnostics, care processes, etc. AI is also making a mark in education by helping the students, faculty members, administrators of education institutions. AI provides a lot of technological advancements in education sector. Such technological advancements have given a mechanism for exploring and predicting future nature of higher education thereby making necessary adjustments in the current trends to cope up with the needs. This chapter discusses the advantages of employing AI in both education and healthcare sectors.

1. Introduction

Artificial intelligence (AI) has various applications and benefits. AI related methodologies are increasing in prevalence in different sectors and is gaining importance especially in healthcare and education sectors.

In health care sector, AI can be applied in patient care, in administrative work, etc., while in education sector AI can make personalization and tutoring in classrooms much easier, it can also help grading work, etc.

AI can do wonders in key healthcare areas such as diagnosing disease. AI algorithms has the potential to help radiologists in detecting cancer. Similarly, AI in education can also be helpful. This chapter thus discusses the advantages of AI in education and healthcare sectors.

The section 2 covers the advantages of AI in education sector, section covers 3 advantages of AI in healthcare, section 4 is discussion and section 5 concludes the chapter.

2. Advantages of artificial intelligence in education sector

There are different advantages of AI in education sector. In this sector, the different advantages will be discussed.

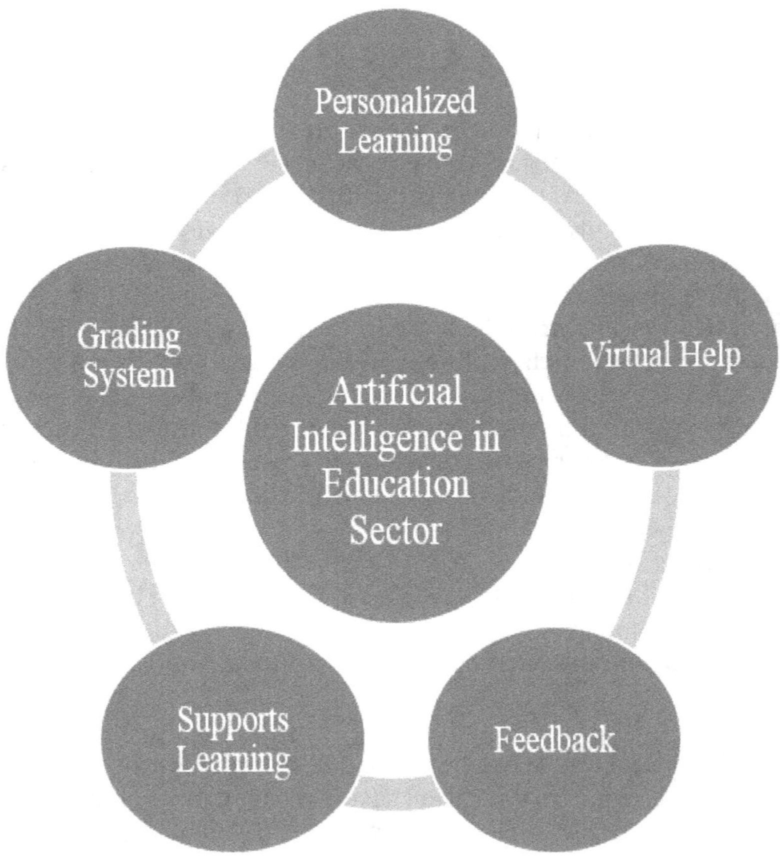

Figure 1. Advantages of artificial intelligence in education sector.

AI in education sector has various advantages which will be explained here. Figure 1 is the representation of key advantages of artificial intelligence in education sector.

2.1 Personalized learning

It is difficult for teachers to personalize study content in a manner that meets the needs of every student in class and give them attention individually. All students in a classroom have different studying pattern. So, it is the need of the hour to develop a system which can monitor the studying pattern of the students and adjust the teaching programme accordingly [7-10].

AI is one such system which can easily adjust to each students' strengths, studying pattern, etc. other factors related to studying pattern which can make teaching- learning effective. AI can help in understanding each students' style and pattern of learning.
Using the knowledge received by going through each students' style and pattern of learning, instructions to be given to each student can be modified and ultimately the study content can be personalized.

2.2 Grading system

Not only study content can be personalized but even grading can become easier with the evolution of AI. Thanks to AI due to which AI based grading is possible. AI can help in grading work. It is easier to grade the students' works and the teachers can get more time for other education tasks in hand [13, 14].

With the evolution of AI, those tasks which were tedious and hectic like that of grading have become easier. AI advantages in education sector are becoming a turning point in education sector.
The main aspect of introducing AI in education sector is to make it easier for teachers to work by helping in different ways and to help students as much as possible. So AI is not only helpful for teachers alone but it is also helpful for students as well.

2.3 Feedback

AI can be helpful in identifying gaps by providing feedback on the basis of the outcome of the result of students in their tests and assessments.

It is a way to confirm that every student has understood the concept. This gives an opportunity for teachers to observe and identify the areas in which students are lacking.

2.4 Virtual help

AI backed applications and systems have the capability to be such designed that they can provide virtual help to students by answering certain questions which are quite often asked to the teachers. Be it basic administrative questions to admission related questions or any study related often asked questions, all these can be answered by AI backed applications or systems.

These systems or applications may answer the questions by convesring in the form of a chatbot, but AI can provide virtual help to students. By doing so, it will be even indirectly helping teachers as it is making their work little easy.

2.5 Supports learning

AI also supports learning by helping in carrying on learning from anywhere. AI backed systems and applications are powerful enough to support learning irrespective of circumstances like pandemic.

Students are attending classes virtually with the help of video conferencing applications or platform. Students are even studying with the help of certain applications or certain study related platforms.

A common factor here in whatever means through which the studies are going on are the role of AI in it. The different applications or platforms through which classes are carried on virtually or whether they help in studying, they are AI backed. Hence, AI supports learning from anywhere, be it any place and any given time.

3. Advantages of artificial intelligence in healthcare sector

AI in healthcare sector has various advantages which will be explained here. Figure 2 is the representation of advantages of artificial intelligence in healthcare sector.

A lot of focus of researchers till now with development of AI in healthcare sector is seen towards diagnosis of diseases. AI can really be of great help in detecting diseases. For example, using AI diagnosis of cancer can be done.

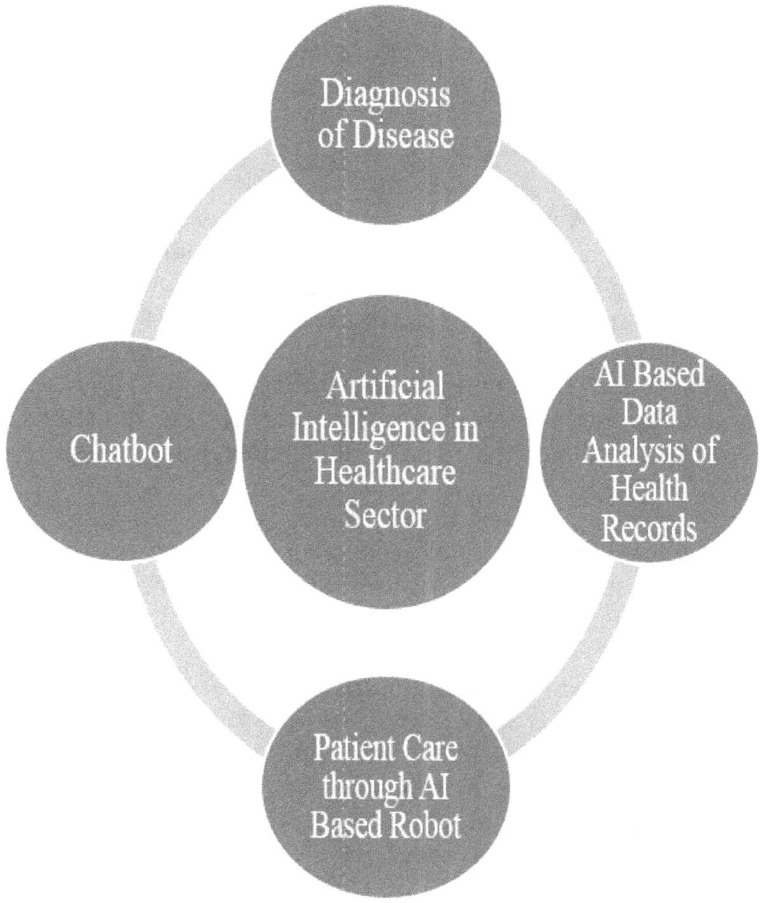

Figure 2. Advantages of artificial intelligence in healthcare sector.

3.1 Diagnosis of disease

The use of AI is done in an important application where it is prevalently visible which is healthcare sector. AI can be helpful in cancer diagnosis. AI techniques can help in early cancer detection. Computer

Aided Detection (CAD) tools are effectively utilized in the cancer detection.

It serves as a platform where the doctor can observe the images and do the initial analysis. It can improve the detection sensitivity and highlight those suspicious areas where there are chances that cancerous cells are present. Not only in cancer diagnosis but also in other healthcare applications AI can be helpful.

3.2 Chatbot

AI based chatbot can be used in healthcare. There are various questions that patients have in their mind. Some of them are basic questions regarding doctor's availability and timing. Also, some basic questions include regarding appointments.

So, to answer such basic questions, chatbot can be used. Doctor's time or any member of the doctor's team handing the basic questions, their time will be saved, and their work will become little bit easier.

On the other hand, chatbot answering their basic questions, patients also sometimes have to wait to get answer to their basic questions. In the case of chatbot, the patients will also not have to wait and will receive immediate response.

3.3 AI based data analysis of healthcare records

Now mostly doctors have electronic health records of their patients. Doctors and health organizations now gather and save electronic health records of their patients as it becomes convenient and useful to maintain electronic health records.

AI based data analysis of healthcare records can be very helpful in patient care. It can provide great information regarding the patient's health based on the health records which will help the doctors in patient care and in deciding the course of treatment.

3.4 Patient care through AI based robot

AI based robot can be used for patient care. Especially during pandemic where social distancing is required, AI based robot can go and give food and medicine to patients. It can even ask health related queries or can even remind the patients regarding the doctors already given instructions. AI driven patient care can transform the healthcare sector for the betterment of people.

4. Discussion

In the chapter above, different advantages of AI in education and healthcare sector are discussed. AI has the capability to benefit the education and healthcare sector which can be seen from the advantages discussed and described in this chapter.

If AI can continue with its capability to benefit education and healthcare sector and provide more advantages to these both sectors in the future, then it will be great for both sectors.

5. Conclusion

This chapter gives a brief overview on the advantages of AI in education sector and healthcare sector. AI has the ability to provide advantages to education sector, thus supporting students, faculty members and administrators in the education sector.

AI is mainly applied for providing personalized learning resources and solutions to students. It is also applicable in assessment and evaluation work.

AI is also capable of providing feedback, virtual help to students and it also supports learning. AI application work in education sector is still developing.

AI based application in education and healthcare sector are still developing. The full consequences of AI development cannot be completely seen today but if AI applications will provide advantages to the education sector and help each person in the education sector, i.e., students, faculty members, administrators then it is likely that application of AI will be encouraged but this all depends on how AI development takes place and how it fares in education sector in the future.

The ability of AI in offering help to support doctors in diagnosing disease is great. In healthcare, AI is helpful in various areas such as diagnosis of disease, helping patients through chatbot, patient care through AI based robot, etc.

Also, AI algorithms can be used in analyzing large amounts of data available through electronic health records which can be helpful. Thus, AI can provide novel solutions to education and healthcare sectors.

References

[1] Richter, O.Z., Marin, V.I., and Gouverneur, F. (2019) Systematic review of research on artificial intelligence applications in higher education-where are the educators? *International Journal of Education Technology in Higher education*, **16**, 1-27.

[2] Rong, G., Mendez, A., Assi, E.B., Zhao, B., and Sawan, M. (2020) Artificial intelligence in healthcare: Review and Prediction case studies. *Engineering*, **6**(3), 291-301.

[3] Popenici, S., and Kerr, S. (2017) Exploring the impact of artificial intelligence on teaching and learning in higher education. *Research and Practice in Technology Enhanced Learning*, **12**, 1-13.

[4] Acikkar, M., & Akay, M. F. (2009). Support vector machines for predicting the admission decision of a candidate to the School of Physical Education and Sports at Cukurova University. *Expert Systems with Applications*, **36**(3 PART 2), 7228–7233.

[5] Adamson, D., Dyke, G., Jang, H., & Rosé, C. P. (2014). Towards an agile approach to adapting dynamic collaboration support to student needs. *International Journal of Artificial Intelligence in Education*, **24**(1), 92–124

[6] Agaoglu, M. (2016). Predicting instructor performance using data mining techniques in higher education. *IEEE Access*, **4**, 2379–2387.

[7] Ahmad, H., & Rashid, T. (2016). Lecturer performance analysis using multiple classifiers. *Journal of Computer Science*, **12**(5), 255–264.

[8] Alkhasawneh, R., & Hargraves, R. H. (2014). Developing a hybrid model to predict student first year retention in STEM disciplines using machine learning techniques. *Journal of STEM Education: Innovations & Research*, **15**(3), 35–42

[9] Aluko, R. O., Adenuga, O. A., Kukoyi, P. O., Soyingbe, A. A., & Oyedeji, J. O. (2016). Predicting the academic success of architecture students by pre-enrolment requirement: Using machine-learning techniques. *Construction Economics and Building*, **16**(4), 86–98

[10] Babić, I. D. (2017). Machine learning methods in predicting the student academic motivation. *Croatian Operational Research Review*, **8**(2), 443–461.

[11] Barker, T. (2010). An automated feedback system based on adaptive testing: Extending the model. *International Journal of Emerging Technologies in Learning*, **5**(2), 11–14.
[12] Casamayor, A., Amandi, A., and Campo, M. (2009). Intelligent assistance for teachers in collaborative e-learning environments. *Computers & Education*, **53**(4), 1147–1154.
[13] Chi, M., VanLehn, K., Litman, D., and Jordan, P. (2011). Empirically evaluating the application of reinforcement learning to the induction of effective and adaptive pedagogical strategies. *User Modeling and User-Adapted Interaction*, **21**(1), 137–180.
[14] Delen, D. (2010). A comparative analysis of machine learning techniques for student retention management. *Decision Support Systems*, **49**(4), 498–506.
[15] Dodigovic, M. (2007). Artificial intelligence and second language learning: An efficient approach to error remediation. *Language Awareness*, **16**(2), 99–113.
[16] Gutierrez, G., Canul-Reich, J., Ochoa Zezzatti, A., Margain, L., and Ponce, J. (2018). Mining: Students comments about teacher performance assessment using machine learning algorithms. *International Journal of Combinatorial Optimization Problems and Informatics*, **9**(3), 26–40
[17] Huang, S. P. (2018). Effects of using artificial intelligence teaching system for environmental education on environmental knowledge and attitude. Eurasia Journal of Mathematics, *Science and Technology Education*, ***14***(7), 3277–3284.
[18] Jain, G. P., Gurupur, V. P., Schroeder, J. L., and Faulkenberry, E. D. (2014). Artificial intelligence-based student learning evaluation: A concept map-based approach for analyzing a student's understanding of a topic. *IEEE Transactions on Learning Technologies*, **7**(3), 267–279
[19] Kardan, A. A., and Sadeghi, H. (2013). A decision support system for course offering in online higher education institutes. *International Journal of Computational Intelligence Systems*, **6**(5), 928–942.
[20] Oztekin, A. (2016). A hybrid data analytic approach to predict college graduation status and its determinative factors. *Industrial Management and Data Systems*, **116**(8), 1678–1699.
[21] Ma, Y., Zhang, P., Tang, Y., Pan, C., Li, G., Liu, N., Hu, Y., and Tang,Z. (2020) Artificial intelligence: The dawn of a new era for cutting edge technology based diagnosis and treatment for stroke. *Brain Hemorrhages*, **1**(1), 1-5.
[22] Esteva, A., Kuprel, B., Novoa, R.A., et al. (2017) Dermatologist-level classification of skin cancer with deep neural networks. *Nature*, **542** , 115-118.
[23] Komeda, Y., Handa, H., Watanabe, T., et al.(2017) Computer-aided diagnosis based on convolutional neural network system for colorectal polyp classification: preliminary experience. *Oncology*, **93** ,30-34.

[24] Ehteshami, B.B., Veta,M., Johannes, V.D.P. et al. (2017) Diagnostic assessment of deep learning algorithms for detection of lymph node metastases in women with breast cancer. *JAMA*, **318** , 2199-2210.
[25] Lee, E.J., Kim, Y.H., Kim, N. et al.(2017) Deep into the brain: artificial intelligence in stroke imaging. *J Stroke*, **19**, 277-285.
[26] Bluemke, D.A.(2018) Radiology in 2018: are you working with AI or being replaced by AI?. *Radiology*, **28** , 365-366.
[27] Shen, W., Zhou, M., Yang, F. et al.(2015) Multi-scale convolutional neural networks for lung nodule classification. *Inf Process Med Imaging*, **24**, 588-599.
[28] Vieira, S., Pinaya, W.H.L., and Mechelli, A. (2017)Using deep learning to investigate the neuroimaging correlates of psychiatric and neurological disorders: methods and applications. *Neurosci Biobehav Rev*, **74** , 58-75.
[29] Kamnitsas, K., Ledig, C., Newcombe, V. et al. (2017). Efficient multi-scale 3D CNN with fully connected CRF for accurate brain lesion segmentation. *Med Image Anal*, **36** , 61-78.
[30] P. Kandpal, K. Jasnani, R. Raut and S. Bhorge, "Contextual Chatbot for Healthcare Purposes (using Deep Learning),*(2020) Fourth World Conference on Smart Trends in Systems, Security and Sustainability*. pp. 625-634, doi: 10.1109/WorldS450073.2020.9210351.
[31] Shen, Y., Guo, D., Long, F., Mateos, L. A., Ding, H., Xiu, Z., Hellman, R. B., King, A, Chen, S. Zhang, C. and Tan, H. (2021). Robots Under COVID-19 Pandemic: A Comprehensive Survey. *IEEE Access*. Vol. 9, pp. 1590-1615. doi: 10.1109/ACCESS.2020.3045792.
[32] Kyrarini, M.; Lygerakis, F.; Rajavenkatanarayanan, A.; Sevastopoulos, C.; Nambiappan, H.R.; Chaitanya, K.K.; Babu, A.R.; Mathew, J.; Makedon, F. (2021). A Survey of Robots in Healthcare. *Technologies*, 9(8), pp. 1-26. https://doi.org/10.3390/ technologies9010008.
[33] Johansson-Pajala, RM., Thommes, K., Hoppe, J.A. *et al.* Care Robot Orientation: What, Who and How? Potential Users' Perceptions. *International Journal of Social Robotics.* 12, pp. 1103–1117, doi: https://doi.org/10.1007/s12369-020-00619-y

www.ingramcontent.com/pod-product-compliance
Lightning Source LLC
LaVergne TN
LVHW011520200926
848484LV00001B/83

* 9 7 8 1 9 2 2 6 1 7 3 0 9 *